T0271153

Strategic Human Resource Management

The second edition of this popular shortform book provides a concise expert summary of key issues in the theory and practice of the management of human resources (HR) – one of the most crucial drivers of organizational performance.

As human resource management strategies evolve over time, this new edition pays special regard to the HR challenges arising from radically altering contexts – economic, social, and technological. For example, the book examines research reports on the impact of the COVID pandemic and other disruptions to the global world of work. It assesses recent HR initiatives and priorities such as Equality, Diversity and Inclusion (EDI) and the HR implications of remote and hybrid working. The book evaluates contemporary critiques that HR practice and research can be part of the problem. In sum, the book offers a route map through the extensive terrain of contemporary research project findings.

Serving as a unique researcher's guide, this concise book enables readers to develop their own ideas for future research and such is essential reading for management scholars and reflective practitioners.

John Storey is a Professor of Human Resource Management at The Open University, UK.

Patrick M. Wright is the Faculty Director of the Center for Executive Succession in the Darla Moore School of Business at the University of South Carolina, USA.

State of the Art in Business Research
Series Editor: Geoffrey Wood

Recent advances in theory, methods, and applied knowledge (alongside structural changes in the global economic ecosystem) have presented researchers with challenges in seeking to stay abreast of their fields and navigate new scholarly terrains.

State of the Art in Business Research presents short form books which provide an expert map to guide readers through new and rapidly evolving areas of research. Each title will provide an overview of the area, a guide to the key literature and theories and time-saving summaries of how theory interacts with practice.

As a collection, these books provide a library of theoretical and conceptual insights, and exposure to novel research tools and applied knowledge, that aid and facilitate in defining the state of the art, as a foundation stone for a new generation of research.

Emergency Services Management
A Research Overview
Paresh Wankhade and Peter Murphy

Cultural Management
A Research Overview
Chris Bilton

Ethical Consumption
A Research Overview
Alex Hiller and Helen Goworek

Strategic Human Resource Management, 2e
A Research Overview
John Storey and Patrick M. Wright

For more information about this series, please visit: www.routledge.com/State-of-the-Art-in-Business-Research/book-series/START

Strategic Human Resource Management

A Research Overview

Second Edition

John Storey and
Patrick M. Wright

Routledge
Taylor & Francis Group

LONDON AND NEW YORK

Second edition published 2023
by Routledge
4 Park Square, Milton Park, Abingdon, Oxon, OX14 4RN

and by Routledge
605 Third Avenue, New York, NY 10158

Routledge is an imprint of the Taylor & Francis Group, an informa business

First edition published by Routledge 2019

British Library Cataloguing-in-Publication Data
A catalogue record for this book is available from the British Library

Library of Congress Cataloging-in-Publication Data
Names: Storey, John, 1947- author. | Wright, Patrick M., author.
Title: Strategic human resource management : a research overview / John Storey and Patrick M. Wright.
Description: 2nd edition. | Abingdon, Oxon ; New York, NY : Routledge, 2023. | Series: State of the art in business research | Includes bibliographical references and index.
Identifiers: LCCN 2023008678 (print) | LCCN 2023008679 (ebook) | ISBN 9781032427836 (hardback) | ISBN 9781032427850 (paperback) | ISBN 9781003364276 (ebook)
Subjects: LCSH: Personnel management. | Strategic planning.
Classification: LCC HF5549 .S8786 2023 (print) | LCC HF5549 (ebook) | DDC 658.3/01--dc23/eng/20230303
LC record available at https://lccn.loc.gov/2023008678
LC ebook record available at https://lccn.loc.gov/2023008679

ISBN: 978-1-032-42783-6 (hbk)
ISBN: 978-1-032-42785-0 (pbk)
ISBN: 978-1-003-36427-6 (ebk)

DOI: 10.4324/9781003364276

Typeset in Times New Roman
by MPS Limited, Dehradun

Contents

List of figures   vi
Acknowledgement   vii

Introduction to the Second Edition   1

1 Mapping the field of strategic human resource
   management   4

2 Strategic human resource management and
   performance outcomes   18

3 Key practice areas and the key levers   32

4 HR competences and the HR function   48

5 The changing contexts of strategic human
   resource management   62

6 Fit, flexibility, and agility   75

7 A stock-take and promising avenues for future
   research   88

References   98
Index   120

List of figures

3.1 The cycle of HR practices   33
3.2 Idealized model of HR planning   35
3.3 Key elements of a performance management system   39
4.1 HR competency model for HR professionals   54
4.2 Nine dimensions of an effective HR department   57
4.3 Waves of HR value creation   60

Acknowledgement

We want to thank Dave Ulrich for his valuable contributions – most especially to the analysis of HR competencies and the HR function in Chapter 4.

Introduction to the Second Edition

The main aim of this second edition of *Strategic Human Resource Management: A Research Overview* is to provide a succinct analytical guide to the extensive body of research in the named field. We have used our experience to survey and evaluate the significant contributions to the main research journals and international conference proceedings. We seek to equip readers with a helpful guide and route map through an extensive terrain of research projects and findings. In sum, this short volume provides the reader with an accessible overview of the field and serves as a guide to developing ideas for future further research.

Theorizing and practice in strategic human resource management do not happen in a vacuum but always within a context, often a dynamic context. Political, economic, legal, and social environments greatly affect the conduct of, and thinking about, SHRM. Since the publication of the first edition of this book in 2019, the turbulence in these multiple contexts has been experienced on an enormous scale. Much commentary in the intervening years has frequently referred to the 'unprecedented' nature of the scale and nature of the unfolding events. Indeed, the short period between the publication of the first edition of this book (2019) and this current edition (2023) has been a period of exceptional turbulence. The effects of a whole series of interrelated changes in context have yet to be worked through and these uncertainties present interesting challenges for new research. Significant developments in the domain of work and employment have included disruptions to the global order stemming from the war in Ukraine, economic turbulence, industrial unrest, political turmoil, and a global pandemic.

The coronavirus (COVID-19) which swept the globe did indeed trigger unprecedented policy and behavioural responses. The pandemic spread with such speed and with such intensity that governments worldwide were impelled to introduce numerous and extensive restrictions on movements and gatherings – known in general as lockdown laws. These laws led to empty places of work, working from home (or indeed 'working from

DOI: 10.4324/9781003364276-1

anywhere') in cases where that was feasible, and ultimately, to many workers re-evaluating their attitudes to work and employment.

A great deal has been written about the impact of COVID-19 on jobs, work, the economy, and society. We review this body of research in Chapter 5 which focuses on the changing contexts of human resource management. The repercussions were many and varied. They include disruptions to supply chains not least because of prolonged and extensive lockdowns in China which were imposed over a number of years. The war in Ukraine exacerbated international supply chain disruptions and generated a crisis in energy supplies with extensive consequences for trade and inflation across the globe. Talk of a 'new normal' suggests potential for lasting changes. There have been a number of new research contributions which have sought to interpret these and similar issues and in this new edition, we report on these.

A notable strand of new research has focused on the HR implications of diverse forms of financing. This has especially been the case with regard to business start-ups, but it is also relevant in cases of takeovers and mergers. Recent research data offer new insights into the role of public and private equity finance, angel investors, venture capital, hedge funds, leveraged buyouts, peer-to-peer lending, green financing, Islamic finance, and so on. Representative of this avenue of research is the work of Di Pietro et al. (2022). They explore different kinds of entrepreneurial financing and their implications for HR practices. A kind of counterfactual can be found in employee-owned businesses and partnerships such as the John Lewis Partnership where managers, claimed that freedom from the demands of the stock market gives them extra scope to take a longer-term perspective (Salaman and Storey 2016). Indicative of the turbulent environment, John Lewis directors in March 2023, began to consider disrupting the 100% employee owned model by seeking some degree of private equity.

Another development has been a series of recent articles in HR journals which critique the role of HRM itself. A number of these suggest that HR has been at times part of the problem rather than part of the solution. A related line of critique, not new but resurgent in the past two or three years, has been the idea of placing HR in the wider frame of multiple layers of economics and politics. This perspective leads to new analyses of conflict and of industrial relations.

Not all changes impacting on work can be placed at the door of COVID. Advances in technology alongside wider social changes find expression in new forms of work and by implication in the management of such work. For example, remote working presents challenges for HR. Ideas about a universal basic income and shifts in psychological contracts carry significant implications for HR. Extensive data and analysis from across Europe have recently become available and merit close analysis – for example, *Living and Working in Europe* (Eurofound 2022).

The interrelated themes of Equality, Diversity and Inclusion (EDI) have continued to attract research attention since the publication of the first edition. Indeed, they have grown in intensity especially with regard to issues of race and gender. Likewise, increasing attention has also been given to the place of neuroscience in HRM and to the implications and role of HRM in relation to the green and sustainability agenda (see Chapter 5).

High-performance work systems have been a key concept in SHRM and as such were covered in our first edition; in this, we review the latest contributions to the literature. One aspect to note is that in the intervening years, the concept has been reassessed often with an even more critical eye – examples include Kirkpatrick and Hoque (2022) and Kim et al. (2021) and yet the same period has seen some interesting refinements to this theme as we reveal in Chapters 2 and 6.

Signalling theory has been, and is, influential in microeconomics but it is new to HRM. It suggests that HRM policies only really have salience when signals sent by managers are coherent and consistent and that these signals are appropriately received by workers. This line of research seeks to dig deeper into the actual *processes* of HR action and impact. For example, it is argued that 'signals will have greater strength and effectiveness if they possess the qualities of salience for receivers, clarity, consistency, frequency and intensity' (Guest et al. 2021). Signals have long been recognized as important in the area of recruitment and selection, but recent research extends the approach to the wider domain of HRM.

Most HR research has tended to focus on managers and their strategies and practices. A recent strand of research has switched focus to view the phenomenon from the employee perspective. Examples include: Beijer et al. (2019) 'The turn to employees in the measurement of human resource practices: A critical review and proposed way forward', and Gold and Smith (2022) *Where's the 'Human' in Human Resource Management? Managing Work in the 21st Century.* Related aspects of this call for refocusing include requests for increased attention to be paid to disability (Bacon and Hoque 2022) and the analyses of bullying at work (Hu et al. 2022).

In summary, the themes outlined above indicate how the second edition of *Strategic Human Resource Management: A Research Overview* is enhanced and brought up to date with the inclusion of new research reflecting new emergent theorizing in the context of key social and economic changes relevant to SHRM.

1 Mapping the field of strategic human resource management

Human Resource Management (HRM) has become the predominant term to describe the theory and practices relating to the way people are managed at work. In previous times (and indeed even now in some places), other terms have been used which, in varying degrees, broadly correspond. These other terms include personnel management, personnel administration, people management, employee relations, human capital management, industrial relations, and employment management. Each of these terms reflects the diverse antecedents of HRM, and they also reveal aspects of the different ideologies associated with these approaches. For example, some early forms of personnel management had a 'welfare' parentage, while others carried traces of a social-psychological 'human relations movement' history (Mayo 1949). Each of these traditions reflected a primary focus on individuals and small groups. Conversely, the terms 'industrial relations' and 'employment relations' reflect the collectivist (pluralist) approach to management–worker relations which, at times and in places, were dominant throughout much of the 20th century in Europe, North America, and beyond (Clegg 1979; Dunlop 1958; Flanders 1964, 1970; Fox 1974). This tradition was taken forward and extended in North America and elsewhere with ideas about mutual gains and union-management partnerships (Kochan and Osterman 1994). The disciplinary roots of the field include aspects of labour economics, industrial sociology, psychology, and law. Some recent reviews of the field have provoked controversy about the appropriate emphases to be given to these disciplines (Troth and Guest 2020; Kaufman 2020). Thus, while Troth and Guest seek to defend the contribution of psychology, Kaufman in his commentary mounts a critique of the negative consequences of the 'psychologisation' of the field – especially in relation to strategic human resource management (SHRM).

The term 'SHRM' is used to emphasize the strategic character of a particular approach to talent and organization management – though some commentators would argue that HRM itself is inherently

DOI: 10.4324/9781003364276-2

strategic in nature. Hence, the terms HRM and SHRM are often used interchangeably.

Two broad streams of research and analysis developed from the 1980s onwards: 'employer strategies' and 'labour movement strategies' (Doellgast et al. 2021). As these reviewers noted:

> While many of the same researchers contributed to both streams, each placed a distinct analytical focus on employer or labor strategies and actions. Both streams also continued to develop through an ongoing debate between pluralist and radical or critical perspectives.
>
> (Doellgast et al. 2021: 559)

The field of HRM/SHRM has burgeoned over the past 30 years. Its roots can be found in American literature of the 1980s, which re-framed people issues away from conceptions that cast people management as an after-thought that could be handled in an ad hoc, reactive way, or managed through formal institutions such as collective bargaining and regulation (Beer et al. 1985). In place of this traditional conceptualization, there was a shift towards a strategic conception that posited workers as 'assets' rather than 'costs' (Storey 1992). The workforce from this perspective was therefore a 'resource' and recognized as a key source (arguably *the* key source) of competitive advantage. As such, these assets were to be treated seriously: the composition planned with care, selected with care, trained and developed, and above all, induced to offer commitment. Indeed, the overall shift was memorably described as a journey 'from control to commitment' (Walton 1985). Alongside all of this, and indeed providing an economics underpinning to it, the concept of 'human capital' came to the fore (Becker 1964).

This reconceptualization coincided with the emergence of the 'resource-based view' in the strategy domain (Wernerfelt 1984; Grant 1991; Peteraf 1993). Emphasis was given to the importance of maintaining a link between business strategy and human resource strategy. The human resource approach displaced 'personnel management' and gave emphasis to the importance of establishing both vertical and horizontal alignment in HR policies and practices.

In the 1980s, influential new models and frameworks were developed including the Harvard Model (Beer 1985), which established a flow from the environment to business strategy and to human resource choices and onwards to outcomes. In parallel, important contingency models and frameworks emerged (Fombrun et al. 1984; Kochan and Barocci 1985; Schuler and Jackson 1987), which made links between appropriate HR strategies and a firm's location in relation to such contingencies as business stages and variations in product/service characteristics (e.g., low cost, innovation, or service quality). Empirical research traced how major mainstream companies and public sector organizations were responding to these ideas (Storey 1992). The role of general managers and line managers alongside human resource and personnel/IR specialists was assessed.

This theme of the nature of the HR function's profile was elaborated and developed by Ulrich in a series of influential publications (Ulrich 1997, 1998; Ulrich et al. 2017). Based on global research, his classification of the HR function into different segments: business partners, shared services, and centres of expertise became the dominant model among practitioners. A related development in the field has been the impact of SHRM on firm performance (Wright and Snell 1998).

A reincarnation of many of the underlying premises of HRM can be found in the influential work of economists investigating the sources of productivity (Bender et al. 2018; Bloom and Van Reenen 2007; Bloom et al. 2012; Sadun et al. 2017). This body of work takes a step back and asks which, if any, 'management practices' impact on productivity. They use the World Management Survey which has been administered across 34 countries (see https://worldmanagementsurvey.org/). They make the case for recognizing the vital importance of management competence, central to which is the competent management of human resources. The key practices are identified as: target setting, the use of incentives, monitoring of performance, and talent management. Achieving managerial competence 'requires sizable investments in people and processes' (Sadun et al. 2017, p. 122). This new wave of research and associated practical interventions replays many of the core themes in classic HRM.

Some recent research has begun to switch the focus from a unit of analysis based around individual firms, to a framing that brings into focus wider 'eco-systems' comprising networks of interdependent individuals and organizations (Roundy and Burke-Smalley 2022; Snell et al. 2023). These networks may operate as hybrids of market and firm relationships.

The above paragraphs give a synoptic view of the emergence and development of the field. Now, we proceed to dig deeper.

Defining the field

Based on a review of SHRM theorizing and research, Wright and McMahan (1992) defined SHRM as 'the pattern of planned human resource deployments and activities intended to enable an organization to achieve its goals' (p. 298). They noted that this entails vertically linking the strategic management process to HRM practices, and horizontally creating coordination and congruence among those HRM practices. They suggested that the major variables of concern in SHRM are, the determinants of decisions about human resource practices, the composition of the human capital resource pool (i.e., skills and abilities), the specification of required human resource behaviors, and the effectiveness of these decisions given various business strategies and/or competitive situations.

(pp. 298–299)

It is important to emphasize that currently the term 'HRM' is used in two different ways. In one usage, which we can term the *generic*, it is used to encompass all of the forms of employment management in its infinite variety. In this first sense, it is just a new label for personnel management or employment management in general. But there is a second usage. In its second form, the term has at times denoted a *particular* approach to employment management. Thus, the term in this second sense refers to one of the many ways of managing labour and is used to demarcate it from other ways. Not surprisingly, the existence of two different usages has caused considerable confusion in the academic literature with commentators often talking at cross-purposes.

So, what is this second, more specific and narrow meaning? In this particular sense, it has been defined as follows:

Human resource management is a distinctive approach to employment management which seeks to achieve competitive advantage through the strategic deployment of a highly committed and capable workforce using an array of cultural, structural and personnel techniques.

(Storey 2007, p. 7)

The definition points first of all to the distinctive means through which objectives will be sought. These include, crucially, the element of a 'strategic' approach. This means that the management of people and of the workforce in general is approached not in an *ad hoc*, tactical, and merely reactive way but in a manner which regards this aspect of management as of central importance. HRM practices helped deliver strategic objectives. Different strategies require different employee skills. As with other aspects of the definition, the interesting features are in noting not only what this form of HRM is, but also what the meaning suggests HRM is not. The counterfactual is important. For the HRM, debate and the emergence of HRM only makes sense when it is recognized as part of the history of its time.

HRM emerged at a time when labour management, in broad characterization, might be described as a secondary, Cinderella-like, management practice ('Personnel Management' was often described in these terms). Markets were defined, finance arranged, and production plans drawn up – and only then was the request for certain units of labour issued, often at short notice. Similarly, as industrial conflict was of concern in the post-second world war period, the skills in subduing and 'managing conflict' were to the fore in the then field of personnel/IR management. It was into this climate when western product markets were coming up against the international competition – and often losing out – that this 'new' approach to managing labour emerged and presented a challenge to existing assumptions and practices.

Second, the definition refers to the deployment of a 'highly committed and capable workforce'. This is an important feature of the distinctive approach. As we know, very large sections of the economy operate on very different principles. The high-commitment approach is relatively unusual in large swathes of the employment scene. Hire and fire, short-term contracts, even zero-hour contracts, outsourcing, agency work, and many other such methods to treat labour as a mere transaction are relatively commonplace. Recent talk of 'employee engagement' or 'employee experience' can be seen as a latter-day attempt to (re)capture some of that high-commitment agenda. The distinctive high commitment mode of HRM equates with what is termed the 'High Road' approach to employment management. The 'Low Road' approach relates to the precarious forms of employment (Osterman 2018). The links between high pay/high productivity versus low pay/low productivity models have been explored in the disciplines of economics (Abowd et al. 1999) and employment relations (Holzer et al. 2004). HRM, in the distinctive sense, is expressive of the High Road approach. This high road/high commitment perspective is likewise integral to the theory of 'High-Performance Workplaces' (Appelbaum et al. 2000) and High-Performance Work Systems (HPWS) (Becker and Huselid 1998) along with the idea of identifiable 'bundles' of HR practices (MacDuffie 1995).

Third, the 'array of cultural, structural and personnel techniques' refers to the mutually reinforcing ways in which a truly thought-out strategic approach can deploy a wide range of methods that would have an internal 'fit' and would complement each other (a further instance of the strategic nature of the idea). These techniques include attempts to: 'win hearts and minds' rather than merely enforce a contract; to deemphasize custom and practice in favour of instilling values and mission; pluralism is also downplayed in favour of an implied unitary perspective where employers, managers, and employees are seen to share at least one similar interest: to keep the enterprise in business. Thus, a set of beliefs and assumptions underpin this *distinctive form* of HRM. Other dimensions stress the role of strategy in that the business plan becomes pertinent to the way that employees and workers in general are managed; and an emphasis on the role of line managers as crucial to the practice and experience of HR policies. Then there is a set of key levers such as serious attention to selection (in place of hire and fire), performance-related pay, an attempt to move from 'temporary truces' in labour negotiations to management through culture, and shared goals.

When viewed holistically, is this package to be regarded as a 'soft', 'human relations', approach with employee welfare at its core? There are facets such as an emphasis on training and development and the winning of hearts and minds that might lean in that direction. But there are also 'hard' aspects to this model of HRM (Storey 2007). Labour is seen as a strategic resource. As such it is to be planned for, measured carefully, and used as an asset. HRM sits alongside the resource-based view of the firm as strategic perspective on how to manage the employment relationship (Storey 1992, 2007).

What about practice? While the HRM label has become so ubiquitous and has, in the main, replaced personnel management in many organizations (contrary to expectations and indeed contrary to empirical evidence during its early days – as revealed by the Workplace Employment Relations Survey (WERS) surveys), the management of work has, over the past couple of decades, not been a steady journey to the wider diffusion of the best practice HRM model. In the wider, generic sense, HRM continues, but the nature of its practice is very varied. This variation is reflected in terms such as 'High Road and Low Road' practices, 'polarized work', and in the metaphor of the 'hourglass economy'. These variations might seem to suggest the degree of strategic *choice* facing HR professionals. Yet, research across major economies indicates that, for many workers, the erstwhile trend towards good practice has shifted into reverse (Kalleberg 2013; 2018).

Theory and practice

As currently conceived, HRM is constituted by both research and practice. These two are related, but they are not the same. It is a truism that practice often differs from theory in the sense that everyday practices do not always live up to some theoretically derived prescription of an ideal or a 'best' way. But the practice-research distinction can be exaggerated. Much research in HRM is simply the identification and cataloguing of practice. For example, they include statistical and descriptive summaries of the state of play with regard to what human resource specialists do, how they are distributed, what influence they exercise, and so on, which are research-based mirrors of practice. The same can be said for those examples of HR research that draw a picture of recruitment and selection practices, appraisal methods, reward systems, and the like. This type of research reflects practice. It is descriptive.

But there is another type of research that seeks to identify 'good practice' and even 'best practice'. This type tries to identify the causal links between context, practices, and outcomes. For example, this goes beyond describing what HR professionals do and moves on to study the impact of what they do on key outcomes such as employee well-being or business performance. The theory then explains why these outcomes might occur by building conceptual frameworks. As a result, it follows that in many instances, actual practice will often differ from 'theory'. Yet additionally, many practitioners pay regard to research when seeking to develop their practice and so theory and practice can become closer as a consequence.

Thus, the question 'what is HRM?' can then be answered in terms of both theory and practice.

The nature of strategy in HRM

A *strategic* approach to HR could normally be expected to include elements such as a longer-term perspective; a concern with big issues that go beyond operational detail; an approach which scans, and factors-in, relevant information about the environment and about changes within it; the construction of policies which seek to align HR practices to the needs of the business often expressed as mission, vision, strategy, or goals; and the construction of HR policies which bring each of the elements of HR into mutual, reinforcing, and alignment. Thus, decisions in relation to recruitment and selection priorities should be consistent with priorities in the areas of goal setting, performance management, reward, training and development, and promotion and exit.

So, whereas an *operational* decision might be confined to a one-off interaction with an employee (for example, how to handle a particular appraisal interview) and may require some tactical skill, SHRM is concerned with the wider issues and usually involves making choices about matters which will have longer-term consequences and will affect the success or otherwise of the business.

The alignment of HR components has been termed 'internal fit', while the alignment of HR with business strategy and the wider business environment has been termed 'external fit'. Strategic HR should aspire to both types of fit (Miles and Snow 1994).

SHRM is concerned with both policies and practices. Ideally, these work in tandem, but appropriate policies can be undermined by poor practices, and conversely, good practice may, to some extent, compensate for defective policies. It is a field that comprises practice, prescription, and empirical study. Although one might desire and assume a strong connection between these, in reality, there is sometimes a considerable disconnect between these three elements.

An important question is who generates HR strategy? It might be a specialist HR Director and team but not all organizations have these. Even if the senior business team has created a separate HR function (in the form of a unit or department), it is possible that they may not necessarily devolve all big decisions in this area to that department. Indeed, the choices about whether to have such an HR department can be seen as one of the strategic decisions we are talking about here.

Research evidence suggests that key integrated business decisions (which include HR and finance and marketing strategies) are formulated by executive groups (not Boards) and that the members of these groups multitask and are most effective when they adopt a business orientation and not a functional orientation. A business orientation 'makes strategic decision makers comfortable to deal with issues outside their business function' (Kelly and Gennard 2007, p. 114).

Classic definitions include the idea that 'business strategy' is:

> The determination of the basic long-term goals and objectives of an enterprise and the adoption of courses of action and the allocation of resources necessary for those goals.
>
> (Chandler 1962, p. 13)

Thus, from one perspective, strategy requires systematic rational assessment of contexts and resources.

Some approaches to doing strategy focus mainly on finding the optimal space or location in a market. So, these approaches tend to look outwards to the characteristic features of a market such as price, quality, and the distinctiveness of offers for goods or services.

A business strategy (and by extension an HR strategy) that focuses more on utilizing internal resources than on locating the best market position is known as 'the resource-based view' (RBV). This was advanced most fully by Prahalad and Hamel (1990) and Grant (1991). These analysts were mainly talking about business strategy but their approach has profound implications for HR. The re-focusing on internal resources is an approach that is closely aligned with the idea of an HRM strategy because it gives emphasis to the importance of leveraging resources to gain a competitive advantage. As noted above, it regards labour as assets rather than in the conventional accounting view as costs. And, of course, one implication of this is that one tends to invest in and to nurture assets, whereas one normally tends to try to cut costs. This idea of the workforce as assets gets to the heart of many approaches to SHRM. It involves seeking to build human capability and to gain competitive advantage from workforce skills, creativity, and commitment.

Strategy as plan?

Another issue that has been central to debates in business strategy and also has much relevance to HR strategy is whether a 'strategic approach' requires a formal plan. There is often a tendency to think about strategy as requiring the compilation of information and as a formal process of decision-making that culminates in a series of plans. But there is another view; the view that suggests strategy can be inferred from a pattern that emerges from a long series of decisions, even in the absence of a formal written plan or strategy document. This could be termed a 'de facto strategy'. This idea of an 'emergent strategy' is normally associated with Henry Mintzberg (1978).

So, an enterprise may have no formal strategy document and yet still have a de facto emergent strategy. Or it may even be that an enterprise has a formal and lengthy strategy document that is largely ignored in practice while a different de facto strategy is pursued.

A de facto strategy which has been built up incrementally and found to 'work' (in the sense that the organization has proved to be sustainable and no major chronic problems are occurring) may add up to a coherent strategy.

But not all ad hoc approaches have such optimal outcomes. '*Ad hocery*' may result in a lack of forethought, inconsistencies, short-term thinking, and waste and can be very costly and lead to an uncompetitive position (e.g., paying redundancies as a reaction to economic downturn and then facing recruitment difficulties and training costs when upturn occurs). The word 'rudderless' is sometimes used to describe this kind of drift and lack of direction. Hence, this particular approach would be considered as non-strategic.

So, what would an approach to HR look like if it was not ad hoc, rudderless, and reactive? The implied alternative is some kind of strategic approach – that is, one which:

- tries to build a big picture
- has a sense of direction of travel
- has some coherence and consistency
- has mutually reinforcing elements

Coherence is about fit and integration. In other words, it suggests that the parts or elements fit together smoothly rather than contradict each other or lean in different directions. A classic example of HR decisions that tend towards contradiction is where 'team focus' is urged and policies are put in place to promote that, but where the remuneration system is based on individual performance-related pay.

But in addition to alignment and coherence of the individual policy components, HR strategy design requires attention to contexts – both inner and outer contexts. A recent special issue of HRMJ places context front and centre of international HRM research (Farndale et al. 2023).

The nature of the design, and the range of factors to be taken into account when attempting this design, is a matter of some debate. The skill involved in making these decisions may be a matter of good judgement – an essential quality for a competent strategist in HR. Some analysts recommend an approach that amounts to a 'design' or 'decision science' (Boudreau and Ramstad 2009) with an associated emphasis on systematic concepts, frameworks, and measurement, while others lean more towards an approach based on aspects of leadership and social intelligence.

Why is SHRM important?

The arguments relating to the importance of SHRM tend to be constructed around the claim that 'people make the difference'. The point being made here is that other resources are available and purchasable (capital, new plant, and new equipment, etc.) on a relatively open market, but it is the creative utilization of these resources and ideas by people (singularly and in combination) which lies at the root of creating a competitive advantage.

These arguments are in some ways similar to those that stress the importance of the resource-based view or of the role of knowledge and the importance of organization capability (Ulrich 1997) or 'dynamic capability' (Teece et al. 1997). The dynamic capability was defined by Teece et al. (1997) as a 'firm's ability to integrate, build and reconfigure internal and external competences to address rapidly changing environments' (p. 516). It suggests that intangible assets, including the knowledge and skills of the workforce, can be configured so that traditional routines do not hamper responses to rapidly changing environments. Instead, more flexible, meta-routines can be created which enable organizations to be capable of a higher state of responsiveness to inherently unpredictable forces. Failure to attract, retain, and motivate the right numbers and right kinds of people mean that opportunities are missed and that other resources are wasted.

In general, the available studies appear to reveal impressive evidence of robust impacts and outcomes (e.g., Huselid 1995; Becker and Gerhart 1996; Ichniowski et al. 1997; Becker and Huselid 1998; Ichniowski and Shaw 1999). An influential idea has been that appropriate 'bundles' of HR practices make the real difference (MacDuffie 1995). These classic studies were mainly conducted in the USA and in the mid-1990s. They suggest that those firms which used 'bundles' of HR interventions were more likely, on a statistical basis, to enjoy better financial performance. This issue of the links between policies and performance outcomes is explored more fully in Chapter 2.

The importance of dynamic capabilities and a strategic mind-set in an innovation-oriented economy heightens the need to attend to the management of human resources and other intangible assets (Davenport et al. 2006). And resource-based theories suggest that sustainable competitive advantage stems from unique bundles of resources that competitors cannot, or find extremely hard to, imitate (Wernerfelt 1984; Barney 1991). Ironically, it has tended to be economists and others who have argued the case that human assets in particular can fulfil this criterion (Polanyi 1966; Davenport et al. 2006; Teece et al. 1997). Such accumulating evidence has helped advance the idea of 'human capital' management.

Contingency models and frameworks

In contrast to the best practice models considered in the previous section, contingency models of SHRM are based on the premise that what is required is a skilful *alignment* between HR policies and various organizational and contextual characteristics. Thus, best-fit approaches can be located within this category. The word 'contingency' here refers to those theories which explain organizational behaviours and outcomes as highly dependent on some inner or outer environmental variable such as country, technology, organizational size or industry type, or the fit with a particular business strategy. In some versions of contingency theory (the more deterministic ones), the interpretation would seem to challenge the idea of strategic choice. In less deterministic versions, strategic choice occurs when HR policies and practices uniquely align to a particular business strategy. Or a contingency such as an organizational context where safety is paramount (Kellner et al. 2023) or special types of workers such as freelancers who require tailored HR practices (van den Groenendaal et al. 2023).

Types of contingency frameworks

Below we summarize four main types of contingency model which link HR strategy to different ways of thinking about context (environment). The four types are: linking SHRM to business strategy; linking SHRM to business life-cycle; linking SHRM to strategy and structure; linking SHRM to social purpose and performance outcomes.

Linking SHRM to business strategy

It is sometimes argued that an HR approach is only 'strategic' if it 'fits' with the organization's product–market strategy and if it is proactive in this regard. Most of the theorists in this category draw on Porter's (1980) distinction between innovation, quality-enhancement, or cost-reduction strategies (e.g., Schuler and Jackson 1987; Miles and Snow 1985).

For example, Schuler and Jackson (1987) suggest that where a firm has opted for innovation as a means to gain competitive advantage, this sets up certain predictable required patterns of behaviour. Prime among these requisite 'role behaviours' are creativity, a capacity, and willingness to focus on longer-term goals, a relatively high level of collaborative action, a high tolerance of ambiguity, and a high degree of readiness to take risks.

Linking SHRM to business life-cycle

The business life-cycle approach essentially seeks to tailor human resource policy choices to the varying requirements of a firm at different stages of its life-cycle, i.e., from business start-up, through early growth and maturity, and eventually on to business decline. At each stage, a business might be hypothesized to have different priorities. These different priorities, in turn, require their own appropriate human resource strategies. There are a number of examples of the life cycle or 'stages' approach (Lengnick-Hall and Lengnick-Hall 1988; Kochan and Barocci 1985; Baird and Meshoulam 1988).

Kochan and Barocci (1985) and others suggest that, at the start-up stage, new enterprises require recruitment and selection strategies that quickly attract the best talent; reward strategies that support this by paying highly competitive rates; training and development strategies that build the foundations for the future; and employee relations strategies that draw the basic architecture and put in place the underlying philosophy for the new business.

Under mature conditions, the emphasis in HRM is upon control and maintenance of costs and resources. Hence, the recruitment and selection stance might be geared to a gradual introduction of new blood into vacant positions created by retirements. There might also be a policy of encouraging enough labour turnover so as to minimize the need for compulsory lay-offs. Meanwhile, the pay and benefits policy is likely to be geared to a keen control over costs. Training and development might be expected to have the maintenance of flexibility and the adequate provision of skill levels in an ageing workforce as their priority.

Linking SHRM to organizational strategy and structure

The most noted example of the strategy/structure linkage of contingency theory is the work of Fombrun et al. (1984). Their model shows a range of 'appropriate' HR choices suited to five different strategy/structure types, ranging from single-product businesses with functional structures, through diversified product strategies allied to multi-divisional organizational forms, and on to multi-product companies operating globally. For each of the five types of situations, the key HR policy choices in the spheres of selection, appraisal, reward, and development are delineated.

For instance, the HRM strategy of a company following a single-product strategy with an associated functional structure is likely to be traditional in appearance. Selection and appraisal may well be conducted in a subjective fashion, and reward and development practices may veer to the unsystematic and paternalistic.

By way of contrast, a company pursuing a diversification strategy and operating with a multi-divisional structure is likely to be characterized by a HR strategy driven by impersonal, systematic devices which are adaptable to the different parts of the organization. Reward systems are likely to be formula based with a tendency towards a focus on return on investment and profitability. Selection, and even appraisal, may be found to vary between the different constituent business divisions.

Linking SHRM to social purpose and performance outcomes

There has been a growing research interest in the issues of Equality, Diversity and Inclusion (EDI). Notably, EDI is often regarded as both a desirable end itself and as a means to other ends such as enhanced organizational performance. A notable phenomenon in recent times has been 'the significant global groundswells of social activism. The Black Lives Matter, #MeToo and LGBTQ+ rights movements have drawn much-needed attention to issues of diversity and the necessity to speak openly about racism and sexism' (Turner and Merrimen 2021). Turner and Merrimen's research tested the link between senior managers' awareness and sensitivity to such issues and the nature of diversity practices. Focusing on higher educational institutions in the USA they found a significant association between the cultural sensitivity of senior HR managers and organizational practices which suggested to the researchers the importance of the discretionary effort of these actors.

A UK-based study of EDI examined how executives in an organization that had developed a strategic business case for diversity and inclusion were able to address the equality implementation gap (between what is espoused and what is achieved) through control over managers in order to direct their actions towards pro-diversity objectives. Interventions such as mandatory diversity training, diversity targets, and diversity monitoring they contend can prompt managers towards making progressive steps but are ultimately limited by management discretion. 'The agency of managers means the equality implementation gap can be reduced but never completely closed' (Noon and Ogbonna 2021: 619).

In tune with both the previous studies, a research project in the USA found 'a virtuous cycle such that increases in board diversity are related to the subsequent adoption of diversity management practices, which are related to subsequently higher levels of board diversity'. They connect board diversity to the adoption of diversity management practices and demonstrate the mutually positive influence they have on each other (Srikant et al. 2021).

Summary

This chapter has summarized the key aspects of SHRM:

- What is it and what does it look like?
- What were its antecedents?
- Why is it important?
- What kind of performance outcomes have been found?
- What are the main theories, trends, and frameworks?

Key issues include:

- That strategy can be emergent as well as planned. Either way, it can be assessed and evaluated in terms of its efficacy and appropriateness to labour and product market conditions.
- Ad hoc decisions and responses which lack consistency may risk inefficiencies and waste.
- HR strategy normally has to validate itself in terms of its contribution to the wider organizational mission. This does not necessarily mean simply following in an unquestioning way the lead taken by other directors in operations and marketing – it may be that a resource-based approach requires a HR strategy which is distinctive.

In the next chapter, we assess the body of research which has tried to clarify the performance outcomes arising from the deployment of strategic human resource practices. These outcomes may be behavioural in the sense, for example, of higher employee commitment or firm outcomes in the shape of higher productivity or even higher profitability.

2 Strategic human resource management and performance outcomes

One of the earliest frameworks for exploring the impact of HR practices on performance was the 'Behavioral Perspective' outlined by Schuler and Jackson (1987) as noted briefly in Chapter 1. Having its roots in contingency theory, this model was based on the assumption that the purpose of employment practices was to shape or control employee attitudes and behaviours. They suggested that (a) different competitive strategies require different employee 'role behaviours', and (b) different HR practices can elicit these different role behaviours. Thus, they suggested that employee role behaviour mediated the relationship between strategy and performance and that HR practices were critical for producing the relevant behaviours. Also central to this model was the need for congruence across HRM practices such that all worked towards producing the required set of behaviours.

The behavioural perspective also formed the basis for Miles and Snow's (1986) exploration of HR practices associated with different organizational types. Having proposed three types, 'defenders', 'prospectors', and 'analysers' in an earlier paper (Miles and Snow 1978), they provided an analysis of the types of practices that would be appropriate for each of these types.

Another behavioural approach to explaining the relationship between HR practices and performance can be found in social exchange theory (Blau 1986; Homans 1961). This theory originated as a way to explain how relationships develop between individuals but was later expanded to explore the relationship between an organization and its employees (Eisenberger et al. 1986). This more macro-level application suggests that when employees perceive that the organization is taking positive beneficial actions towards them, they will reciprocate in positive and beneficial ways towards the organization. Consequently, a number of authors have suggested that commitment-based HR practices demonstrate beneficial treatment of employees, which causes them to reciprocate by being more

DOI: 10.4324/9781003364276-3

committed and productive, resulting in higher organizational performance (e.g., Chuang and Liao 2010; Messersmith et al. 2011; Sun et al. 2007).

While these frameworks provide process-focused explanations for the relationship between HR practice and performance, the resource-based theory (RBT) of the firm (Barney 1991; Wernerfelt 1984) provided a higher-level explanation for why HR practices can impact firm perform- ance. Barney (1991) noted that resources that are valuable, rare, inimi- table, and non-substitutable can be a source of sustainable competitive advantage to a firm. Sustainable advantages accrue when a firm imple- ments a value-creating strategy that competitors have ceased trying to imitate. While such an advantage is defined in terms of economic rents that can be distributed to, or among, a variety of stakeholders (e.g., share- holders, customers, employees, etc.; see Coff 1999), the assumption within empirical research is that such advantages are observed in shareholder returns, and thus financial- and market-based performance of firms.

Early on, debates arose about the extent to which HR practices could be viewed as sources of sustainable competitive advantage, with the debates focused on the inimitability of the practices. Wright et al. (1994) suggested that any HR practice could easily be imitated by competitors. However, Lado and Wilson (1994) argued that the system (as opposed to individual practices) could be unique, causally ambiguous, and syner- gistic in how it impacted firm competencies. Later, Barney and Wright (1998) similarly suggested that while competitors could imitate any one practice, they would find it difficult to imitate the system of practices. Consequently, the field has come to a consensus on the importance of HR practices and their potential to at least aid in creating competitive advantage. This consensus has become so great, that one would be hard pressed to find any study of the relationship between HR practices and performance that does not at least pay lip service to the RBT as the overarching rationale for hypothesizing a positive relationship.

The earliest conceptual and empirical research on HR practices began with explorations of the 'determinants' of the various practices. Miles and Snow (1978) were among the first to offer a framework for aligning HR practices with strategy. They argued that the different strategic types (defenders, etc.) required different approaches to how they managed people. They then provided an analysis showing the different HR practices associated with these strategic types and provided company examples to illustrate these differences. Baird and Meshoulam (1988) explored the determinants of HR practices rather differently. Instead of focusing on business strategies, these authors looked at the different stages in organizational life cycles and provided a conceptual examina- tion of how HR practices might become more sophisticated as firms moved into different stages. Lengnick-Hall and Lengnick-Hall (1988) developed a model juxtaposing organizational readiness and corporate growth potential to create a two-by-two matrix. They then hypothesized the different types of HR systems that would be associated with each.

A more recent two-by-two matrix to describe different systems of HR practices was proposed by Lepak and Snell (1999). Grounded in the Resource Based View (RBV) they proposed two dimensions along which to categorize different talent pools: value and uniqueness. They then suggested that human capital pools within each of the four resulting quadrants would require different approaches and different systems of HR practices.

In line with these conceptual models, the early forms of empirical research explored the determinants, rather than the outcomes, of HR practices. For instance, Snell (1992) was among the first to explore the drivers of HR practices at the organizational level of analysis. He viewed HR practices as control mechanisms (input including selection; and throughput, using for example, behavioural appraisal; and output, using for example, results-based appraisal) and found that the use of these aspects of HR practices was associated with administrative information and strategic context. Snell and Dean (1992) explored the link between integrated manufacturing and HR practices. They measured integrated manufacturing in terms of the use of advanced manufacturing technology, just-in-time inventory control, and total quality management. They suggested that such manufacturing technologies required upskilling of the workforce to be able to effectively utilize the technologies. Thus, they expected that their use would be associated with more selective staffing practices, comprehensive training, developmental performance appraisal, and equitable rewards. They generally found support for these hypotheses among operations staff and quality-control staff, but not among production control employees.

Arthur (1992) examined how strategy impacted HR practices in a sample of steel mini-mills. Using cluster analysis he identified six different clusters of mini-mills similar in their profile of HR practices. He then collapsed them into two types: 'cost-reducers' and 'commitment maximisers'. This was consistent with Walton's (1985) view of firms using control or commitment approaches, and Arthur's (1994) later use of this nomenclature. He found that mini-mills emphasizing manufacturing few products in large quantities tended toward the use of a cost-reducer/control HR system, while those stressing more flexible manufacturing were more likely to use a commitment-maximiser HR system.

Research redirection: HR practices and performance

Following the initial inquiries into the determinants of HR practices, the field then began to shift to exploring the consequences, particularly their impact on firm performance. This research progressed in three stages as described below.

Stage 1: demonstrating the relationship between HR practices and performance

Exploring the determinants of HR practices, while useful, did not accomplish the goal of showing that HR mattered. However, that soon changed. Huselid's (1995) seminal study provided the empirical foundation for HR advocates to argue that HR can have a profound impact on organizational performance. Using a sample from the Russell 3000, Huselid surveyed Chief HR Officers regarding their use of 13, what he termed, 'High-Performance Work Practices' (HPWS). (These can be seen as the component elements of the much vaunted 'HPWS'). He then regressed the firm's financial performance (both Tobin's Q and gross rate of return on assets) on these practices and found significant results. However, the basis for the study's immediate popularity stemmed from the fact that he provided point estimates of the value of HR practices. In fact, he concluded that a one standard deviation increase in the use of HPWS was associated with a *per employee* increase in market value of $18,641, an increase of $27,044 in sales, and an increased profit of $3,814. Needless to say, HR practitioners jumped on these results to tout their importance, and HR academics quickly set out to conduct similar studies.

Appearing somewhat simultaneously with the Huselid (1995) study were three other studies that captured the imagination of the field by demonstrating empirical linkages between HR practices and performance. First, Arthur (1994) used the data from his previously discussed study to examine how HR systems might differentially impact outcomes. His results showed that, compared to mini-mills using commitment-based HR systems, those using control systems displayed lower productivity, higher scrap rates, and higher employee turnover. MacDuffie (1995) examined how bundles of organizational systems impact performance in a manufacturing environment. Using data from automobile assembly plants, he demonstrated that those using a combination of 'high commitment' HR systems and low inventory and repair buffers consistently outperformed those using mass production systems in terms of both quality and productivity. Delery and Doty (1996) tested the relationship between HR practices and performance in a sample of banks. Distinguishing among universalistic, contingency, and configurational approaches, they found the most support for a universalistic (a consistent set of practices across all firms) model in terms of explaining performance variance.

Unsurprisingly, these four studies appearing within a two-year time frame sparked a plethora of further studies examining the relationship between HR practices and performance. For instance, Youndt et al. (1996) followed up the original Snell and Dean (1992) study by surveying the companies regarding a number of performance measures. They found that an HR system focused on enhancing human capital was related to employee productivity, machine efficiency, and customer alignment, but that this relationship was predominantly observed with a quality manufacturing strategy.

But demonstrating a clear link is by no means easy. Based on an empirical study of HR and firm performance in Finland, it was found that the link between HR practices and firm performance was highly equivocal; the stage in the economic cycle was found to play a much more direct part in explaining firm performance (Lahteenmaki et al. 1986).

Stage 2: exploring the black box

As the research base showing a positive relationship between HR practices and performance grew, one thing was missing: an empirical exploration of *how* these practices impacted performance. Wright et al. (2005) described this problem as the failure to explain the 'black box' between practices and performance. Their call, along with others, began to spark an increase in studies that explored the mediating mechanisms between these two variables.

So, for example, Cappelli and Neumark (2001) conducted an interesting study examining the costs and benefits of HPWS. They found that these practices transfer power to employees and result in higher wages, but only weakly impacted productivity. Given the higher wages, they found that there was no effect on labour efficiency in terms of the output per dollar spent on labour. Way (2002) found similar results in a sample of small businesses. His results showed that HR practices were associated with lower workforce turnover, but not with labour productivity.

In a study of call centres, Batt (2002) found that HPWS were negatively related to quit rates and positively related to sales growth and that the impact of HPWS on sales growth was mediated by quit rates. Takeuchi et al. (2007), relying on the resource-based view of the firm and social exchange theory, hypothesized that HPWS raise human capital and social exchange within a firm and that the human capital and social exchange should be related to establishment performance. Using a sample of Japanese business establishments, they found that human capital and social exchange mediated the relationship between HR practices and establishment performance.

In an extensive meta-analysis, Jiang et al. (2012) explored human capital and employee motivation as mediators of the relationships between HR practices and voluntary turnover, operational performance, and financial performance. They found that the skill-enhancing HR practices relationship with financial performance was partially mediated by human capital, employee motivation, turnover, and operational outcomes, but that the motivation- and opportunity-enhancing practices relationship with performance was fully mediated by these variables.

In what Schuler et al. (2014) refer to as 'targeting practices', a number of studies began to emerge which examined HR practices developed specifically to encourage certain behaviours. For example, Collins and Clark (2003) examined HR practices for top managers. They investigated how HR practices that encouraged networking were related to how much top managers networked internally within the firm and externally with others outside the firm. They found that HR practices encouraging networking were related to sales growth and stock growth and that these relationships were mediated by networking behaviour. Similar efforts have explored HR practices targeted at HR flexibility (Chang et al. 2013), customer service (Chuang and Liao 2010), and knowledge-intensive teamwork (Chuang et al. 2016).

Stage 3: process models of the relationship between HR practices and performance

While the mediation research has demonstrated the significance of a number of mediating variables, a further development was the emergence of process models of the relationship. One of the earliest models was proposed by Truss and Gratton (1994). Building on the previous work of Dyer (1985), they distinguished between 'Planned HR Practices' and 'Implemented HR Practices'. They noted that some practices could emerge, not as a result of a planning process, and conversely, some practices that are planned may never be implemented.

Bowen and Ostroff (2004) provided another foundational contribution to process models of strategic HRM through their development of a construct they termed HR 'system strength'. Those authors used communication theory to examine how HR systems could strongly or weakly communicate the intended messages aimed at managing employee behaviour. They argued that climate serves as the critical multilevel mediating construct between HRM practices and performance. They stated,

> We propose that HRM content and process must be integrated effectively in order for prescriptive models of strategic HRM actually to link to firm performance. By process, we refer to how the HRM system can be designed and administered effectively by defining metafeatures of an overall HRM system that can create strong situations in the form of shared meaning about the content that might ultimately lead to organizational performance.
>
> (Bowen and Ostroff 2004, p. 206)

They argued that the *strength* of the HR system can be described as the extent to which the system induces conformity. Consequently, they described the features of an HR system that could create strong situations as having distinctiveness, consistency, and consensus.

Building and expanding on these basic ideas, Wright and Nishii (2013) and Nishii and Wright (2008) proposed a more thorough process model. This recognizes that the basic relationship between HR practices and performance requires a number of individual-level processes. In addition to the distinction between intended HR practices and actual HR practices, they further recognized that the actual practices are implemented by managers, and thus, there could be significant *variance* in the practices across managers, and even across employees with the same manager. The next stage in the process entailed clarifying the *Perceived HR Practices.* Even if a supervisor treats two employees the exact same way, it can be perceived differently by each. The concept of *employee reactions* describes the affective, cognitive, and behavioural responses of employees to the practices they perceived. Finally, how all employees coordinate, integrate, and align their behaviours determines the performance at the unit level. Thus, their process model starts at the unit level, goes down to the individual level, and then comes back up to the unit level.

Similarly, Guest and Bos-Nehles (2014) developed a model of HR practice implementation. They described four stages of implementation. In the first stage, HR managers and senior executives make the decision to implement HR practices. In the second stage, HR managers consider the cultural and regulatory constraints to decide on the quality of the HR practices that can be implemented. The third stage concerns how line managers and/or senior managers actually implement the HR practices. The fourth stage refers to the quality of implementation by line managers.

A recent approach within this process model of the HRM-performance relationship turns to the role of *employee attributions* (Sanders et al. 2021). These authors note that while early research on the HRM-performance relationship failed to explain how the association was achieved, recent work from a process perspective has started to remedy this. This approach examines *how* employees perceive HR practices, *how* line managers communicate and implement practices, and *why* employees believe that management implements specific HR practices (Sanders et al. 2021: 695). For further analysis of HR process research and HR strength see also Sanders et al. (2021).

In an example of this approach, Alfes et al. (2021) explored how the extent to which employees attributed the presence of HPWS to a firm's desire to improve employee well-being, and to a firm's desire to increase performance, impacted employee engagement. In their study of 484 employees across 5 different organizations, they found that HPWS was positively related to both types of attributions, and both types of attributions were positively related to employee engagement. They also found that the two types of attributions interacted significantly to increase employee engagement.

In another project using attributions theory, Katou et al. (2021) conducted a multilevel study with 158 Greek organizations to investigate how line manager implementation of HRM, HR strength, and HR attributions impact organization performance. They found that HR strength (in terms of distinctiveness, consistency, and consensus) fully mediated the relationship between the HRM practices and line manager implementation at the organizational level. They also found that the line manager HRM implementation fully mediated the relationship between HR strength and employee attributions of both the commitment and control orientations of those practices. Finally, they found that employee attributions fully mediated the relationship between line manager implementation and organization performance.

Guest et al. (2021) used signalling theory to analyze HR processes and HR attributions. In a study of 83 bank branches, they found that implementing a coherent set of high-commitment HR practices and having agreement between managers and staff about those practices were related to employee attributions regarding the commitment- or control- based motivation underlying those practices. However, they did not find that the attributions were related to branch performance.

Thus, these process models primarily recognize the fact that the ways through which HRM practices can influence performance require examining processes at multiple levels of analysis. They also correctly note that what an organization *intends* to do according to its HR strategy may diverge greatly from what *actually happens* and how employees experience HR practices (Nishii et al. 2008). The recent research focuses on how employees make attributions regarding why organizations implement practices has helped to enlighten the ways in which these practices may or may not be related to performance.

Having described some of the theories, the more impactful empirical research, and the process models linking HR practices to performance, we now turn our attention to answering the two critical questions: What do we now know about this relationship, and what do we still not know?

What do we know about the relationship between HR practices and performance?

Given the extensive literature on HR practices, one would expect that there would be a number of consistent findings. A more accurate description of this literature, however, is that there are indeed quite a number of findings, but few very consistent ones.

There is a positive relationship between the use of HR practices and unit performance

One almost unarguable finding across the hundreds of research studies conducted examining the link between HR practices and performance is that a positive relationship exists between these two variables. Combs et al. (2006) identified 92 studies with an overall N of over 19,000 that fit their criterion to meta-analyse the relationship between HR practices and performance. Using a conservative estimate, they suggested a mean correlation of 0.20 between HPWS and performance. They noted that while this number may not seem large, 'it is much larger than what is found among other organisation-level phenomena where long-held organisational performance hypotheses either do not stand up to the evidence ... or are much smaller than predicted by theory ... ' (p. 517).

However, in a later meta-analysis, Tzabbar et al. (2017) performed a moderating meta-analysis, comparing their results to those found in past meta-analyses. The moderated aspect of the meta-analysis entailed examining if different characteristics of the study, such as the type of performance measure or the country/region in which the studies were conducted, explain variance in the effect sizes observed. Some of the moderating results will be discussed below, but for now the most important comparison is with regard to the overall effect size. They found a mean z effect size of 0.09 and noted 'the reported association is smaller than the effect size reported in prior meta-analyses' (2017, p. 139).

In addition, recent research has explored the simultaneous effects of HRM practices with other aspects of the employee experience. For example, Ehrnrooth et al. (2021) examined the simultaneous effects of transformational leadership and HPWS on employee attitudes. In a study of 308 subordinates of 76 managers, they found that both transformational leadership and HPWS were positively related to employee self-efficacy, engagement, organizational identification, and turnover intentions. While the effects of transformational leadership were reduced when accounting for HPWS, the effects of HPWS were only marginally reduced when accounting for transformational leadership.

The positive relationship between HR practices and performance transcends country boundaries

Hofstede (1993) has strongly influenced management thinking based on his research on country cultures. He originally described four dimensions of culture: individualism-collectivism, masculine-feminine, uncertainty avoidance, and power distance, and he later added the dimension of long-term-short-term orientation. For decades, authors suggested that US-originated HR systems, such as HPWS, would not work or at least not work as well in certain country cultures. However, Gerhart and Fang

(2005) were among the first to question what they termed the 'cultural constraint' hypothesis which suggests that the effectiveness of HR practices is constrained by country cultures. They noted the conditions that had to be true in order for the cultural constraint hypothesis to hold, and presented preliminary data suggesting that these conditions likely did not hold. Then, in a meta-analysis using 156 effect sizes and over 35,000 firms, Rabl et al. (2014) found (a) an overall mean correlation of 0.28, (b) that the relationship between HPWS and performance was positive in every country, and (c) that the relationship was *actually stronger* in countries that the cultural constraint hypothesis would suggest would result in weaker relationships.

Using meta-analysis, Tzabbar et al. (2017) found that the effect size was positive and significant in all regions and that the effect sizes were largest in Asia, Eastern Europe, and the Middle East.

Bundling of HR practices matters in the relationship with performance

MacDuffie (1995) was one of the first researchers to introduce the concept of 'bundling'. He actually described the importance of bundling a set of HR practices with corresponding production system characteristics, but many readers interpreted his bundling concept to refer mainly to bundles of HR practices. In the Combs et al. (2006) meta-analysis described below, the researchers demonstrate that the effect of a system of HR practices is greater than the effect of individual HR practices. In fact, the average correlation between individual HR practices and performance was only 0.14 compared to the 0.28 estimate for the systems of HR practices as noted above.

Combs et al.'s results were not perfectly mirrored by Tzabbar et al. (2017) who found that while HPWS had a stronger relationship with performance than profit sharing and voice, they did not correlate higher than development, training, and job security practices. One of the unique aspects of their study stemmed from their moderation analyses where they explored how different aspects of the studies might explain variance in the effect sizes observed across studies. They found that societal context explained 33% of the variance such that the highest effect sizes were observed among studies conducted in Asia, Eastern Europe, and the Middle East with significantly lower effect sizes found among studies conducted in Australia, Europe, and North America. The industry sector explained 12% of the variance in effect sizes, with the highest effects observed in low-tech firms followed by service firms with high-tech firms having the lowest observed effect sizes. Finally, firm size explained 8% of the variance in effect sizes with the largest effect sizes being observed among large firms relative to medium or small firms.

What do we still not know about the relationship between HR practices and performance?

While the above conclusions seem almost unarguable given the significant body of research that exists, a number of unanswered questions remain.

Which practices?

While research has clearly demonstrated the positive relationship between HR practices and performance, the critical question remains unanswered: which practices? As early as Becker and Gerhart's (1996) introduction to the *Academy of Management Journal*'s special issue, we see complaints about the lack of consistency in the HR practices measured across the studies. They noted that no single practice was part of each paper, and only one, training, appeared in all but one paper. This problem has not gone away. Posthuma et al. (2013) analyzed 193 peer-reviewed articles and identified 61 specific HR practices that had been measured. However, they bemoaned the fact that there was very little consistency in the practices that have been measured across these studies. Similarly, Langevin-Heavey et al. (2013) found little agreement on the specific practices that have been used in studying the relationship between HR practices and performance.

Recently, Su et al. (2018) have suggested expanding the list of practices used in this research. They noted that since the early distinction between commitment- and control-oriented practices (Arthur 1994), HPWS research has focused almost entirely on commitment-oriented practices, In two studies, Su and Wright (2012) and Su et al. (2018) have found that adding control-oriented practices increases the amount of performance variance explained beyond that of just the commitment-oriented practices.

Moreover, in addition to the question of which practices, there is also little consensus on the approach to aggregating the practices. Since the Huselid (1995) study, virtually all research has simply added the items together to compute an overall scale (or used factor analysis and added up the sub-scales). However, research based on the ability, motivation, and opportunity (AMO) perspective has suggested that HPWS really contain three sub-components: ability-enhancing, motivation-enhancing, and opportunity-enhancing sub-scales. For instance, Gardner et al. (2011) noted that ability-enhancing practices were actually positively related to turnover, while motivation- and opportunity-enhancing practices were negatively related.

More comprehensively, the Jiang et al. (2012) meta-analysis segmented HR practices into three sub-components: AMO-enhancing practices. They found that skill-enhancing practices were more strongly related to human capital and less strongly related to employee motivation than motivation and opportunity-enhancing practices. They noted:

> The findings of the differential relationships between the dimensions of HR systems and organizational outcomes also offer methodological implications for strategic HRM research. First, if all three dimensions of HR systems have unique effects on organizational outcomes, failure to include any dimension may compromise the overall impact of HR systems on organizational outcomes or at least lead to inaccurate results ... . Relatedly, the results indicate that the three-dimensional model fit the data slightly better than the model combining the three HR dimensions into a unidimensional HPWS element.
>
> (Jiang et al. 2012: 1278)

In addition, while most of the research has focused on HPWS, some research has explored HRM practices aimed at more specific outcomes. For example, Salas-Vallina et al. (2021) introduced what they called 'well-being-oriented' human resource management practices (WBHRM), in essence a set of HR practices aimed specifically at ' ... maintaining and improving employees' psychological, physical, and social well-being, on the basis of a positive employment relationship' (2021: 334). They argued that such a system of practices both increases employee well-being while enhancing performance, because people support one another, set ambitious goals, and are willing to go the extra mile. In a study of 2,914 employees across 192 teams, they found that the WBHRM practices related to employee well-being and individual performance and that the effect was accentuated when they experienced engaging leadership. So, research in this area increasingly allows for exploring different *orientations of practices* as well as the basic practices themselves.

Which direction does the causal arrow point?

While the positive relationship between HR practices and performance seems virtually unarguable at this point in the field's evolution, what remains somewhat unclear is whether increasing HR practices causes higher performance or high performance encourages firms to develop and implement more HR practices. Guest et al. (2003) examined the relationship between HR practices and performance among a sample of UK-based firms. They found that while the positive relationship existed between the practice and performance, once they controlled for past performance, the relationship disappeared. Similarly, Wright et al. (2005) found that measures of HR practices were equally correlated with measures of past, present, and future performance and that the correlations between HR practices and future performance were greatly reduced when controlling for past performance. These findings do not suggest that HR practices do not cause future performance; rather they only suggest that current research cannot prove which way the causal arrow points.

How much value can we expect from increasing HR practices?

Given the fact that the data does not prove a causal relationship of HR practices on performance, this calls into question some of the point estimates of the value accrued from increasing them. For instance, Huselid and Becker (2000) stated, 'Based on four national surveys and observations on more than 2,000 firms, our judgment is that the effect of a one standard deviation change in the HR system is 10–20% of a firm's market value' (p. 851).

Likewise, based on their meta-analytic results discussed above, Combs et al. (2006), when trying to argue for why the observed mean correlation of 0.20 is meaningful, state:

It means that 20% of the utility available from predicting performance differences among organizations is given by HPWPs. Increasing use of HPWPs by one standard deviation increases performance by .20 of a standard deviation. For example, Huselid (1995) reports means of 5.1 and 18.4% and standard deviations of 23 and 21.9% for gross ROA (i.e., returns plus non-cash items) and turnover, respectively. In this sample, a one standard deviation increase in the use of HPWPs translates, on average, to a 4.6 percentage-point increase in gross ROA from 5.1 to 9.7 and a 4.4 percentage-point decrease in turnover from 18.4 to 14.0%. Thus, HPWPs' impact on organizational performance is not only statistically significant, but managerially relevant.

(pp. 517–518)

Here again, we do not mean to dispute the relationship between HR practices and performance, nor do we suggest that implementing HR practices should not lead to greater performance, all else being equal. However, we do suspect that there may be a *dually causal* relationship, where HR practices may help increase performance and that increased performance may then provide more money to invest in HR practices. But, in such a situation, using the correlation or effect size reflects both of the causal forces, and thus overestimates the true impact of HR on performance. Thus, given that the causal arrow could point either way (or both), we caution that the point estimates of the value of increasing HR practices may possibly be overly inflated.

Conclusion

Research on the impact of HR practices on performance has grown to be one of the more frequently studied phenomena in the field of HR. This research has been conducted in cross-industry (e.g., Huselid 1995), within industry (e.g., Delery and Doty 1996; MacDuffie 1995), and within corporation (e.g., Wright et al. 2005) settings. In addition, it has been conducted across a large number of geographies. In the main, these studies have revealed a consistent finding of a positive relationship between HR practices and performance. In the next chapter, we make a closer examination of the precise nature of the practices involved.

3 Key practice areas and the key levers

Ultimately, strategic human resource management is defined by what it does: that is, the actual *practice* of SHRM. To put this point another way: 'it is the *how* of HRM in the chain of processes that make the various models of HRM work well or poorly' (Boxall et al. 2008, p. 7).

The critical incidents between entry and exit of workers which attract the attention of HR practitioners include job design and team design, on-boarding and induction, assessment, training and development, engagement, reward and retention, talent management, employment relations, safety, health and well-being, and organizational design and redesign, organizational vision, mission, and culture management. The value of these kinds of activities can best be appreciated when their absence or their mishandling is observed; this can lead to expensive and sometimes even existential threats to an organization. Examples include the passivity of the HR department at Miramax in the face of complaints about Harvey Weinstein; similar passivity in the British House of Commons when faced with complaints from staff about bullying and sexual harassment from some elected members; a failure to have active systems in place at Oxfam resulting in catastrophic reputational damage in 2018; and well-publicized reputational damage to P&O Ferries when in March 2022 they dismissed 800 established staff without notice while replacing some of them with foreign workers on less favourable terms (Calder 2022).

Beyond the universal good practice idea is the potential gained from tailoring the specific practices to organizational strategy – e.g., whether geared to enable a low cost, quality, or innovation business strategy (Schuler and Jackson 1987). So, for example, an innovation-led approach may need to emphasize team-oriented practices (Jørgensen and Becker 2017). Further, such a goal requires practices that allow and encourage engagement and divergent thinking rather than mere conformity to standard HR practices and procedures (Shipton et al. 2016). This, in turn, implies changes to leadership development practices. Thus,

DOI: 10.4324/9781003364276-4

practices must not only be performed well, they need to align. This means vertical alignment with organizational goals and horizontal alignment of practices with each other.

Analyses of its enactment are normally structured in line with a notional chronology from staff recruitment through to exit. See Figure 3.1 which displays the range of HR practices and interventions as a cycle.

If the constituent elements are approached in a *strategic way*, then careful regard will be given to how such activity contributed to organizational objectives. If they are approached in a non-strategic manner, then action will be governed by ad hoc responses or by following some traditional mode of practice.

There is a danger in treating each component as a separate process. This happens sometimes in both theory and in practice. Thus, the HR function is often separated out into sub-functions each staffed by specialists in their own right. Yet, the practices may only add significant value if they are coherent and mutually reinforcing. They contribute best when adding to 'system strength' (Hauff et al. 2017). This is the idea expressed in the notion of 'High Performance Work Systems' (Hong et al. 2017; Meuer 2017) and the concept of 'HR bundles' (MacDuffie 1995) as described in the previous chapter.

Thus, pursuing a particular strategic goal – such as innovation – will carry implications for the kind of HR practices that should be pursued. An example, based on the target of encouraging innovation, can be found in research conducted at European Centre for Nuclear Research (CERN) (Mabey and Zhao 2016). This emphasized the value of trust, of rewarding knowledge sharing, encouraging diversity, and fostering communities of practice.

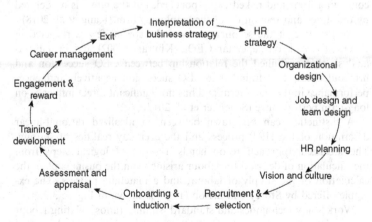

Figure 3.1 The cycle of HR practices.

In the realm of practice, HR departments are likely to require cooperation from line managers and will benefit from enhancing their implementation skills (Trullen et al. 2016; López-Cotarelo 2018).

We start the analysis with planning and resourcing.

Human resource planning and resourcing

If the mantra 'people are our most important asset' is to mean anything, then the methods used in the selection of the workforce would need to be taken seriously rather than in the *ad hoc* and peremptory fashion so often used in the past, and to a lesser extent, today. The process ideally begins with a careful assessment of the organization's needs with regard to size and composition of the workforce. From there, it would proceed through recruitment and selection. The throughput continues with deployment and succession planning, and on to various modes of exit including redundancy, retirement, voluntary exit, and enforced exit: all part of the process of labour flow, in, through, and out.

There appear to be fashions in human resource planning (HRP). A decade or so ago 'talent management' and 'high potentials' were key themes. But a recent assessment has argued that the focus on 'special talent' has 'passed its prime' and attention now shifted to more 'inclusive models' (Tavis 2018). This is a contentious claim as a significant body of research suggests that a minority of high performers account for a disproportionate amount of value gain across many organizations (Ready et al. 2010; Aguinis and O'Boyle 2014). As a result, star performers are subject to invitations to defect to competitor organizations and thus employers tend to take steps to protect these resources. A study of financial analysts showed that star performers are indeed attractive to competing firms and risked being poached, but the effect is moderated by the status and reputation of the employing firm (Kang et al. 2018).

An example of the scepticism about the special few is reflected in Khurana's work on superstar CEOs (Khurana 2002) and in a meta-analysis that examined the relationship between CEO succession and firm outcomes. This found that CEO succession negatively influences performance in the short term and has no significant direct influence on long-term performance (Schepker et al. 2017).

A distinction can be drawn between an idealized rational-linear description of the HRP process and the everyday realities of staffing. The idealized approach recommends a series of logical steps from the calculation of demand for labour arising from the business plan, the calculation of the supply of labour, and a matching process. The example offered by Storey and Sisson (1993) is shown in Figure 3.2.

Work study techniques and standard 'staffing ratios' relating labour requirements to indicators such as the number of assembly lines and

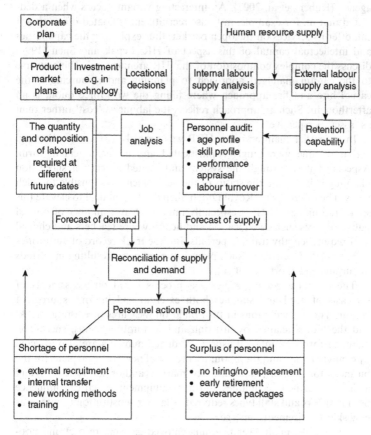

Figure 3.2 Idealized model of HR planning.

Source: Storey and Sisson 1993, p. 113.

shifts to be worked, the number of beds on a hospital ward or the number of children in a school may all be used as part of the calculation. Career planning and succession planning can also be used as part of this stock and flow approach.

The planning stage may be more complex than is at first apparent. Not all workforce requirements are necessarily met through direct employment. Services may be outsourced to agencies or to self-employed workers. There may be staff working in-house in a manner dedicated to one organization even though these staffs are actually employed by an agency (Rubery et al. 2002). An interesting variant occurs when a dedicated unit in, for example, in-house recruitment is floated off so that it can offer its services on the open market, thus exploiting the capabilities and intellectual capital of this aspect of HR. Lepak and Snell (1999) discuss the complex composition of the 'HR architecture'. The converse to the careful managed approach to planning and resourcing is the casual hire and fire approach where filling the workforce quota is an afterthought. Such an approach reflects the labour as 'cost' rather than as 'asset' perspective.

In an earlier manifestation, HRP was termed 'manpower planning' and it became increasingly sophisticated and mathematical in form. Aspects of flow through the system and related aspects of succession planning helped raise the status of the departments responsible for such plans. The oil company Royal Dutch Shell did a great deal to elevate this set of techniques. HRP is especially important in a number of critical public services such as education and health where teachers and clinical staff require lengthy training periods. But the track record of authorities responsible for delivering such plans has been poor, resulting in periods of surplus and shortages of staff.

The formal approach suggests a process based on assessments of forecasts of need and supplies both external and internal sources of labour. These calculations in turn build on measures of existing 'stock' and the 'flows' shaped by attrition and maturation. Thus, succession planning forms an integral aspect. Predicted numbers are also affected by changes in demand for labour as a result of new strategic plans for the business (for example, entry into new markets and/or new functions) and as a result of new techniques and new equipment which can influence both numbers and skill types required as labour substitution occurs or as new skill requirements emerge.

For a while, manpower planning enjoyed growing respect and popularity. But this was followed by a decline as the mechanistic nature of the models and their associated plans became seen as detached from reality (Cowling and Walters 1990). While the full potential of manpower planning was rarely realized in actual practice, the basic components such as measuring employee turnover and retention became well-established as core personnel management tools. In subsequent years, these tools and techniques, in adapted form, became more fully developed in desktop computer personnel information packages and the idea of Human Resource Information Systems (HRIS) – software combining multiple forms of information – became popular and there remains considerable interest in their potential (Bersin 2016). Such modern versions can differentiate more between jobs and occupations and be geared to both organizational and employee outcomes (Schmidt et al. 2017). In any case, other research shows that only supportive career management approaches have an impact on performance outcomes (De Vos and Bart Cambré 2017).

An area that has attracted considerable research within the realm of HRP has been that of 'career management'. During the classic years of formal HRP, this often meant planned progression through a corporate hierarchy and the associated aspects of 'succession planning' (Mayo 1991). Many consultancies still offer this service. For example, they may offer to assess 'bench-strength' – that is an organization's preparedness to replace key staff. But, in general, as corporations downsized and fragmented, the ownership of career management seemed to shift from the organization to the individual. Concepts such as the 'boundaryless career' came under scrutiny (Arthur and Rousseau 1996) along with 'portfolio careers' (Arnold 1997). There are two broad views on the state of play. One suggests that the abandonment of organizational careers has not been as dramatic as often suggested (Guest and MacKenzie-Davey 1996). An alternative view is that the growth of precarious work has severely dented career management along with training and development.

Recruitment and selection

Following the process of HR planning and the identification of the staffing requirements implied by the business strategy, it may be necessary to recruit new staff to posts – either externally sourced or recruited internally. Recruitment is the process of generating a pool of candidates. It is followed by a process of selection between these candidates.

It has been claimed that the staffing function, including recruitment and selection, is 'the most critical human resource function for organizational survival and success' (Collins and Kehoe 2009, p. 209). For knowledge-based firms such as digital enterprises, financial services, and pharmaceuticals this is especially critical. But it can also be crucial in other settings including retail, hospitality, and other industries which rely heavily on the behaviour of customer-facing staff. It has been argued that as organizations are made up of different groups of employees, employment systems, including recruitment, need to match their approaches to these characteristics. In other words, recruitment and selection systems need to be tailored to these groups; hence, there is no single best recruitment system. Requirements for knowledge, skills, and abilities (KSAs) will vary across occupations to reflect differences in task complexity and task interdependencies (March and Simon 1958; Thompson 1967). This perspective offers a view of organizations as comprising different groups or subunits each with their own organizational design needs and staffing requirements. Some units can be shielded from uncertainty and this allows routine and standardization of tasks. Staff resourcing can reflect this. Conversely, other roles are exposed to high levels of uncertainty and these require special resourcing approaches. This leads to the identification of appropriate recruitment strategies (Collins and Kehoe 2009).

External recruitment may be by open advertising followed by selection processes including online tests, assessment centres, and interviews. But part of HR strategy in some organizations has been to tailor resourcing to particular groups and sources. Thus, in the UK, the much expanded fast food and coffee shop industry tends to recruit using employment agencies and to gear recruitment to young enthusiastic labour from European countries such as Spain, Portugal, and Poland. Similarly, UK cruise ships tend to recruit their cabin and catering staff almost exclusively from India and the Philippines. These staff are recruited by agencies in Mumbai and elsewhere and are allocated a fixed-term renewal contract for tours of duty.

This kind of arms-length contracted approach does not suit all situations. The move towards in-house direct labour was undertaken for a reason. Control of a total labour force and the desire to instil commitment may impel managers to categorize at least certain segments of the labour force as permanent staff with a sense of identity and commitment to the employer brand. Internships have become a significant method of recruitment especially for graduates (Hao and Liden 2011).

Following recruitment and selection, a further HR intervention is likely to include some form of performance management.

Performance and reward management

The term 'performance management' suggests an interconnecting set of policies and practices which have as their focus the enhanced achievement of organizational objectives through attention directed towards individual and group behaviour. Its elements normally include setting clear goals and objectives, formal monitoring of performance, and the use of outcome reviews to attempt to shape future behaviour (London and Mone 2009). The management of individual and group performance is elevated to a matter of strategic importance. As such, a formal 'performance management system' may be constructed. An example is shown in Figure 3.3

This suggests a continuous cycle formed by establishing a clear linkage between the corporate and business strategies to the identification of departmental objectives and from there on to individual objective setting. Ideally, organizational objectives and individual employee behaviours should be aligned. This sets up the possibility of performance evaluation in terms of prime organizational objectives and, from there, implications can be drawn for what kinds of feedback, rewards, and development processes should be put in place. Thus, finding a way to allow differential rewards may be part of a performance management

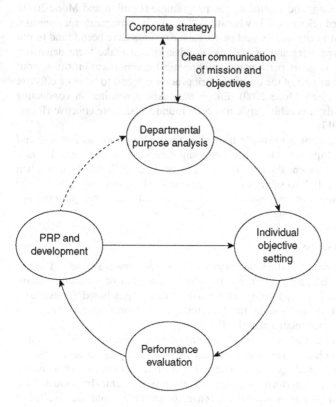

```
                    ┌─────────────────────┐
                    │  Corporate strategy │
                    └─────────────────────┘
                              │
                              │   Clear communication
                              │     of mission and
                              │        objectives
                              ▼
                      ╭───────────────╮
                      │  Departmental │
                      │ purpose analysis │
                      ╰───────────────╯
```

Figure 3.3 Key elements of a performance management system.

Source: Storey and Sisson 1993, p. 133.

system but that is only one element of a larger objective. In some instances, development may be a bigger aim than assessment. Clarity and specificity in goal setting are important (Locke and Latham 1990). Feedback can be a problematic process; it needs to avoid comments on personal characteristics and to focus on specific behaviours and goal progress (Kluger and DeNisi 1998). Critical elements are perceived fairness and equity (Giles and Findley 1997).

Other key issues for practitioners in operating a performance management system include the need to elicit the active buy-in of executives and managers to the design and use of the programme, linking the components of the programme to overall organizational strategy and to each department's priorities, keeping the programme current, capturing the learning, and evaluating the programme (London and Mone 2009). Perceived relevance is key because off-the-shelf instruments for appraisal tend not to engage. Annual performance reviews have been found to put both appraisers and appraisees on edge and to make them defensive. Instead, ongoing performance-enhancement communication throughout the year as part of the ongoing work process is found to be more effective (London and Mone 2009). Either way, skill is required in conducting appraisals; a coaching style has been found to be more effective (Russo et al. 2017).

Assessment is normally framed as for both performance review and for development. There is an ongoing debate about the control versus the development dimensions. The process is complicated further when there is a link to salary or bonus payments. Research suggests that the involvement of employees in agreeing the fairness of the performance measures is vital (Groen et al. 2017).

Compensation

Compensation is the monetary side of the total reward system. The key issues addressed by researchers concern the types of monetary reward and their impact. Two main types are structured pay based, for example, on skill or location in the hierarchy, and second, various forms of performance-related pay (PRP).

'Reward' includes various monetary-related elements such as pay and benefits plus various non-monetary aspects including intrinsic rewards. The whole package is often referred to as 'total reward'. Reward choices are: base pay, performance pay, or indirect pay/benefits. Individual, team and/or organization-wide rewards are, for example, profit sharing. Taken together, 'total reward' includes monetary compensation (including cash and benefits) and non-monetary rewards (Gerhart 2009). Settling on a monetary reward often depends on the 'going rate' for similar jobs in similar labour markets. Firms may have more discretion over *how* they pay (that is, what form compensation takes, especially with regard to pay for performance) rather than *how much* to pay (Gerhart 2009).

Payment by results (PBR) is one form of PRP. It was common in industries such as engineering and textiles where paying by the piece was normal. From the 1980s onwards, there was an expansion of PRP into non-traditional areas such as banking and the civil service. Overall, there has been a shift from job evaluation-based pay structures to more PRP methods.

There are two sub-types of PRP: linking pay to performance as measured by the achievement of specific outcomes such as units produced; and assessing performance in terms of behaviours as in merit rating derived from assessment of traits such as problem-solving, cooperation, and the use of initiative. A meta-analysis of incentive effects of individual PRP revealed a productivity effect of around 30% (Locke and Feren 1980). But other research shows how PRP systems deteriorate over time and how the effect only works in the context of straightforward physical tasks. Also interesting is the 'sorting effect' – that is, the way in which the existence of a PRP attracts some workers and repels others (Lazear 2000).

Part of the drive in the direction of PRP in the 1980s onwards was the intent to individualize the employment relationship and break away from standard collective contracts. But PRP schemes seem counter-productive as the link between performance and pay becomes subject to anomalies. Individual PRP can conflict with attempts to forge teamwork and there is a danger that the focus on individual reward compromises other incentives and sources of work motivation (Gerhart 2009).

Individual PRP systems can also undermine team-based management approaches. Thus, PRP as with any reward system has to align with other features of the organizations. The idea of 'fit' is also relevant in relation to other aspects of HR policies such as high organizational commitment and organizational citizenship and with intervening variables of ability, motivation, and opportunity (Appelbaum et al. 2000). For example, with regard to opportunity, group-based incentives are more likely to be relevant in small group settings rather than in larger group settings (Kruse 1993).

Alternatives to individual PRP include group performance schemes and organization-wide profit-sharing schemes. An alternative is 'gain-sharing' which is based on the sharing of cost savings and may also be used in cases of productivity gain sharing (Kruse et al. 2010).

Finally, with any form of PRP, there are likely to be measurement issues. Results-based measures may seem more directly linked to effort and ability but there are also grounds for using behaviour-based methods. These can take into account judgements about surrounding factors and wider forms of contribution such as customer service and colleague support. But, on the downside, there may be deficiencies in rater reliability (Viswesvaran and Ones 1996).

Human resource development and talent management
Strategic training and development are concerned with the design and implementation of training and development systems to successfully impact organizational performance (Noe and Tews 2009). It is argued that there need to be clear links between business strategy and the design and delivery of strategic training and development initiatives. Likewise, the evaluation of these efforts should lead to feedback into the business strategy (Tannenbaum and Woods 1992).

Managerial commitment to training is often indicative of a wider commitment to a workforce; it sends a message about the value invested in employees. Conversely, the absence of training may indicate a wider message about the undervaluing of staff. Thus, investment in human resource development (HRD) may be associated with a desire for a high-skill, high-value, and high-pay strategy as opposed to a low-skill, low-value, and low-pay equilibrium. As part of this, dynamic training not only adds skills but can also help to attract and retain staff.

Some analyses suggest that HRD needs to be tailored to the different occupational groups that normally make up an organization (Lepak and Snell 2003). Thus, routine training in standards and conformity may be geared to contract employees fulfilling routine tasks whereas commitment and values-based development may be offered to core knowledge workers. There are complications because professional staff may be oriented to commitment beyond the organization and this has implications for HR practices (Olsen et al. 2016).

It is argued that talent management, and HRD more generally, is especially important in an age of globalization and an increased reliance on knowledge workers (Guthridge et al. 2008; Beechler and Woodward 2009). Organizational success becomes more dependent on finding, keeping, and deploying the right people (Boudreau and Ramstad 2005; Boudreau and Ramstad 2009). Hence, developing and utilizing the appropriate talent management system becomes ever more important (Sparrow and Makram 2015). Further, while the issues of managing talent are universal, they are especially acute in emerging market economies (Glaister et al. 2018) where talent shortages highlight a pressing need for organizations to adopt strategic approaches. Moreover, survival in a rapidly changing and global context requires the nurturing of 'dynamic capabilities' (Easterby-Smith et al. 2009). Such a perspective aligns with human capital and the resource-based view of the firm (Barney 1991).

There is a question concerning who owns the responsibility for skill development. Is it the state, the organization, or the individual? Or a combination of these? In so far as the organization plays a part there are further questions about the role of the HR/training department and the role of line managers. A survey in the United States found 57% of training and development professionals outsourced all or part of their training (Johnson 2004). Yet, the growth of the corporate universities phenomenon suggests a desire to own and control this important function and a belief that training and development merit a strategic intervention (Taylor and Storey 2016).

For many managers, training and development simply do not represent strategic issues, rather they are regarded as secondary and even a luxury. In contrast, a learning organization puts learning and knowledge at its centre and uses them as a fundamental regenerating resource

(March 1991; Nonaka and Takeuchi 1995; Davenport and Prusak 1998). Using a similar logic, social networks and social capital are recognized and used as important resources for knowledge creation and sharing (Nahapiet and Ghoshal 1998). A recent meta-analysis revealed a significant performance improvement effect both for individuals and groups tied into networks. They further show the benefit of making use of bridging roles which span different social networks (Brennecke and Stoemmer 2018). Likewise, it has been argued that talent management focused on social networks has a positive outcome (Glaister et al. 2018).

At a level beyond individual training and development, HR may contribute to the goal of embedding 'organizational learning'. This is an abstract concept based on the idea of organizational culture and practices which encourage the creation, sharing, and retention of relevant knowledge. To a degree, the simple experience of working jointly on a common purpose can be expected to enhance organizational learning. Thus, the generation of routines can be a form of organizational learning (Argyris and Schon 1981; Easterby-Smith et al. 2009; Argote and Miron-Spektor 2011).

Employment relations, employee engagement, health, and wellness management

When considered from a strategic HRM perspective, employment relations (also sometimes termed industrial relations or employee relations) can be regarded as representing a series of choices about how to engage with workers either directly or by working with their representatives. These latter may be trade unions or representatives of employee associations. So, one set of choices might be whether to recognize trade unions at all and, if so, to what extent and for what purposes. For example, whether to recognize one or more unions for collective bargaining purposes with a view to reaching collective agreements. From this, many other options ensure – for example, what will be the bargaining units, will negotiations extend across different locations, who will be involved? If unions are not involved then will some form of staff association be used for consultative purposes?

These choices are usually heavily context dependent. Changing contexts are often associated with shifts in power dynamics – a central concept in the IR perspective. Employment relations differ from other aspects of SHRM in that it tends to be more explicit in its recognition of the *plurality of interests* in work organizations. Industry sector, time, and place all make a difference in this dynamic of interests and power relations. A few decades ago, the predominant mode of representation would have been through trade unions. Pay and other conditions of employment were mainly settled through collective bargaining. Over the intervening years, the picture has changed dramatically.

In the UK, the Trade Union Congress (TUC) Directory 2018 reports that union density in the private sector was 13.4%, while in the public sector it stood at 52.7%, and the overall figure was 23.5%. Government statistics show the rate declined further to 23.1% in 2021 - the lowest rate ever recorded in comparable data (DBEIS 2022). The salience of industrial relations issues facing most managers today is far less than it was some decades ago. Context differs also in relation to the laws governing employment matters in different economies.

Nonetheless, the strategic question of what kind or relationship with the workforce is to be sought remains to be addressed. Where unions or staff associations exist, most managers will simply have inherited this situation and will need to decide how to handle it. Will the strategy be to marginalize the representatives and to try to communicate with the workforce as individuals, or will some form of partnership arrangement be attempted? Formal relations may be pursued as a means to institutionalize conflict and manage discontent or more ambitiously they may be used to seek mutual gains through productivity agreements (Flanders 1964).

As Kochan and colleagues showed, US firms such as Ford and General Motors found it easier to engage the workforce in programmes of HRM change when they involved the unions and removed a source of mistrust. From here it was a short step to various modes of partnership agreements with the unions (Kochan et al. 1986).

A feature of part of the current industrial relations scene is the concern about precarious employment in the form of skewed employment contracts (such as zero-hour contracts) and even the absence of employment contracts when self-employment and agency work systems are deployed. In the UK, the government responded to pressure by commissioning an inquiry into 'modern employment practices' including the so-called 'gig economy'. The Taylor commission reported in 2017 in a report entitled '*Good Work*'. The review's stated goal was that 'all work in the UK economy should be fair and decent'. However, it also stated a belief that the 'British way' of flexible labour markets works and that the aim should be to build on the distinctive strengths of the existing framework of regulation. It recommended, however, that reforms be made to tax status, the minimum wage, zero-hour contracts, and agency work, along with changes to rights and benefits; information and consultation; and enforcement and tribunals (Taylor 2018).

Beyond formal industrial relations, a key agenda item in recent years has been to foster 'employee engagement'. This term has become central to the lexicon of many managers and consultants and a quasi-industry has been built around it. Much of the popular literature on the subject is superficial but the idea has remained active for a number of years now. A distinction is often made between its use as a psychological state and employee engagement as a set of practices designed to encourage employee commitment (Truss et al. 2014). It has been argued that engagement is dependent on trust and supervisory support (Holland et al. 2017). Attempts to measure engagement have often been problematic (Shuck et al. 2017). From a more traditional IR/HRM perspective, Purcell offers an assessment of the employee engagement fad. He is critical of the lack of rigour underpinning many of the claims within this approach but holds up the prospect of finding some potential value within the approach by 'build[ing] on the key advantage of the focus on employees, their beliefs, values, behaviours and experiences at work in a way not seen before in mainstream HRM or employee relations' (Purcell 2014, p. 253).

An extension from the usual engagement agenda geared towards productivity has been a focus on health and well-being in many workplaces. This includes work on stress management, safety, and even happiness. Ironically, there may be tension here. Engaged workers exhibiting high organizational citizenship behaviour may be prone to burn-out and stress (Conway et al. 2016; Deery et al. 2017; Kilroy et al. 2017). And yet, research in the NHS reveals that engagement may offer a win–win for employers and employees: a 'virtuous circle'. 'There is clear evidence that trusts with higher engagement levels have lower levels of sickness absence among staff, and also have lower spend on agency and bank staff'. The size effect was substantial – a one standard deviation increase in overall staff engagement is associated with a £1.7 million saving on agency staff costs for the average trust (Dawson and West 2018).

Organization design: structuring and 'organizational culture management'

The ways in which tasks and functions are divided and arranged, activities grouped and coordinated, and lines of accountability drawn form the basis of job design and organizational design. This design activity is by no means solely the responsibility of HR specialists but they may have an input into these choices. Likewise, HR strategists may be involved in the vision, mission, values, and culture dimensions.

Examples of changes to organizational forms which also normally carry a culture aspect include downsizing, decentralizing, devolving, and divisionalising and the general drift towards semi-autonomous business units. Structures are often neglected in analyses of HR, yet the way work is organized into units of accountability is very important. The consequences of the broad move away from the large corporate firm with its multiple layers, job evaluation techniques, and career progress have been extensive. There would seem to have been a shift from bureaucratic forms to 'new' forms such as networks (Miles and Snow 1986), cluster organizations (Quinn 1992) virtual organizations, and hypertext organizations (Nonaka and Takeuchi 1995). The overall theme is one of fragmentation, enterprise, agility, and a greater emphasis on a shift to market-facing units.

An early move from the large corporation was the process of divisionalising. This was prominent in the 1990s (Marginson et al. 1995). Early examples of divisionalisation were found in Du Pont and General Motors early in the 20th century (Chandler 1962). The later phase allowed greater focus, clarity, and accountability. It also allowed financial and cost accounting tailored to specific business areas. This laid the basis for an 'enterprise' cultural perspective.

A related shift was towards marketisation. One aspect of this was to externalize (outsource) activities that were formerly performed in-house. This occurred within both public and private sector organizations. This carried implications for HR in that the numbers of workers directly employed decreased and much of the responsibility for labour management was itself outsourced. The idea was to retain core competency functions. Even where functions remain nominally within a unified organization, a quasi-market was created by means of a purchaser-provider split in public service organizations. Services were 'commissioned' and purchased in an 'internal market'. This could lead to a shift from an employment relationship to a contract for services type of relationship.

The broad shift from proceduralism and collectivism to a more individualist approach with an aim to engender commitment is itself a sign of a significant culture change. The wider political, social, and economic contexts impelled this shift. The move from mass employment in heavy industries to a service-based economy, where customer responsiveness became crucial, moved vision, mission, and culture change to centre stage. The baseline is the idea of an organization's ultimate and enduring purpose (beyond surviving and making a surplus). 'Strong cultures' were extolled in the *In Search of Excellence* movement (Peters and Waterman 1982) – though dysfunctional companies have also been noted to have been misled by strong cultures albeit of a negative kind.

Beckhard points out that managing culture change is not just a matter of managerial will and communication. It is inextricably linked with structural conditions including external conditions that might make the status quo unsustainable. His change management guidelines highlight the importance of building a critical mass of support and a willingness to commit resources into the change programme. He outlines a series of steps: the design of a future state, a diagnosis of the current state, identifying what needs to be done to move including the sorts of relationship required, formulating how an organization will function under the desired state, and the switch of behaviours including those of senior managers (Beckhard and Harris 1987). These ambitious forms of intervention are likely to include, but go beyond, the inputs from HR specialists. They need to be aligned with the array of supportive mechanisms – the key 'levers' – reviewed throughout this chapter.

Conclusion

This chapter has offered a synopsis of some of the large body of research on the wide array of SHRM practices. Inevitably, the coverage of those literatures is only indicative. Lots of research evidence is omitted, but in broad measure many of the ongoing debates about the choices facing SHRM practitioners are reflected in the chapter. There are aspects such as social capital and the encouragement of building and benefiting from networks that are crucial yet not conventionally covered in most considerations of HRM practice areas. It is also noteworthy that HR practices and philosophies are subject to significant shifts over time. Economic cycles appear to have a significant impact on these as do more structural shifts such as globalization. Hence, for example, soft HRM processes may not be resilient in recessions (Cook et al. 2016).

In the next chapter, we take a different perspective by examining in more detail the nature of the competencies which underpin effective strategic human resource management and we look more closely at the HR function itself.

4 HR competences and the HR function

In this chapter, we turn to an examination of research on the strategic contribution of the HR function itself. By 'function' here, we refer to the institutionalized forms which HR practice takes – usually in the form of some kind of departmental structure. Thus, we discuss the capabilities and competences of those who provide HR services (including both policy and practice) and we look at how the HR function is organized (e.g., centralized or decentralized; fragmented into separate sub-units or integrated; outsourced or in-house). There is a two-way relationship between HR ideas and the HR function. Emergent and dominant ideas shape the function's form and function; conversely, HR practitioners help shape ideas even if they do not always fully determine them. Research from Finland indicates the link between HR capabilities and the adoption of HR practices (Beletskiy and Fey 2021)

A complicating factor is that while larger employing organizations tend to have specialized and dedicated HR departments, many small- and medium-sized enterprises operate without them. In these latter circumstances, general managers and other management specialists undertake the tasks involved in managing human resources. Indeed, even in large corporations which have their own HR departments, some of the major strategic choices about the management of the human resource may be taken by influential senior managers from other disciplines such as chief executives, works managers, production directors, or finance directors (Storey 1992). Furthermore, even when HR specialists do exercise influence by shaping policy, the actual realization of these policies in everyday practice usually depends heavily on the role of line managers (Trullen et al. 2016; López-Cotarelo 2018).

There have been attempts to professionalize this domain of management, but there has been limited success in achieving occupational 'closure' of the kind associated with the traditional professions (Abbot 1988). Accordingly, HR work is undertaken by general managers, as well as professional specialists, and by hybrid managers who have multiple

DOI: 10.4324/9781003364276-5

responsibilities. Most of the research on HR competences is restricted to those who self-define as specialists.

The chapter is organized as follows. In the next section, the backstory of how today's HR function emerged is summarized along with an outline of the main areas of research and debate. Then, in section two, the focus shifts to a closer consideration of HR competences. Section three examines recent developments in the organization of the HR function.

The backstory

From the earliest days of HRM in the 1980s, there has been discussion about the capability of personnel departments to translate conceptual models into actual practice. As we have seen in earlier chapters, the conceptual models emphasize strategic and integrated approaches. With respect to the personnel (or HR) function, the questions arising therefore included the extent to which such prescriptions were being followed and how the function was responding.

In some formulations, this was turned into a question about the 'impact' of HRM ideas on personnel as a function (Sisson 2001). However expressed, the underlying questions concerned the extent to which the prescriptive models were being adopted by personnel specialists and their ability to deliver these. To an extent, this acknowledges that HRM ideas emerged from outside the HR function.

Many of the early reports and analyses were sceptical about the degree of adoption. Tyson and Fell (1986) identified different categories and types of personnel managers. 'Clerks of works' were largely involved in routine matters such as record keeping and handling documentation. 'Contracts managers' tended to handle industrial relations matters in workplaces with trade unions. 'Architects' were involved in policy making and were senior managers who tended to identify as business managers first and personnel managers second. They concluded that, in practice, the 'clerks' and 'contract manager' types well outnumbered the 'architects'. Likewise, Sisson (1995) recorded 'little impact' of HRM on personnel in the 1980s and early 1990s. Using data from the well-regarded Workplace Employment Relations Survey (WERS), he updated the analysis and amended the judgement to one of 'partial impact' (Sisson 2001). The WERS data revealed a mixed picture: there was little increase in board-level representation for the personnel/HR function, and rather than an integrated, holistic approach being widely adopted, the evidence pointed to the function remaining fragmented and 'balkanized'. On the other hand, the much anticipated externalization of the function (to outsourced suppliers) had not occurred to any significant extent during this period. Based on additional survey work, Caldwell (2003) reached similar conclusions while also noting the ongoing 'ambiguities and uncertainties' in the role of personnel management/HR.

As observed, one of the claimed distinctive features of the new approach was a greater focus on strategy rather than merely efficient administration of the workforce. This strategic element relates to both a tighter horizontal integration so that the various sub-elements of the function align (e.g., recruitment with training and with compensation and promotion), and a tighter vertical integration so that as a whole these elements align with the business strategy. This ambitious mission for HRM requires appropriate competences and appropriate organizational arrangements – i.e., the two themes that form the main focus of this chapter.

Findings from the WERS in the UK based on data from 2,680 workplaces using very detailed face-to-face administered questionnaires with multiple respondents, again suggested 'little evidence of an increasingly strategic role for HR' between the 2004 survey and the one conducted in 2011 (Van Wanrooy et al. 2013). The percentage of workplaces belonging to organizations with a formal strategic plan for employee development was 56% – not significantly different from the survey in 2004. Details of the study can be found via this link: www.gov.uk/government/publications/the-2011-workplace-employment-relations-study-wers.

In the USA too, there have been some sober assessments of the nature and contribution of the HR function. Most infamous was the extended essay *Why We Hate HR* (Hammonds 2005). Among a number of critiques this argued that HR had essentially focused on administrative work which was being outsourced; unfortunately, the HR function, he argued, was ill-suited to the remaining crucial element, the strategic role. Lawler (2005), as well as Becker and Huselid (2006), reached a similar conclusion. Later in this chapter, we present some alternative data and interpretations.

Analysis in the USA of small- and medium-sized enterprises drawing on the National Organizations Survey revealed a positive unit-level performance effect from having a formal HR function (Chadwick and Li 2018). One explanation is that their presence may prompt and promote the creation and maintenance of a high-performance work system. Useful though such evidence might be, such studies shed little light on the actual *processes* involved. The relative lack of data about the processes involved in doing HR – that is, the 'black box' between policies and outcomes – as has been noted by a number of observers including, for example, Haggerty and Wright (2010). Their work emphasized the importance of implementation rather than formulation and linked this to crucial attributes such as legitimacy and visibility of the HR function. These attributes may be problematic even with regard to receptivity by fellow managers, never mind the wider body of employees (Haggerty and Wright 2010, p. 112).

There have been limited studies of the ways in which outsourcing HR activities affect the HR role internally, its remaining competences or its influence with senior management. One study, that compared HR departments which had engaged in HR outsourcing with those departments which had maintained full in-house HR provision, found that the latter enjoyed more positive outcomes such as enhanced trust, more competency development, and a clearer strategic focus (Glaister 2014). The enhanced benefits of an in-house HR function are also underlined by the findings from a study of a German subsidiary of a US company. This revealed that the effects of outsourcing on the in-house HR function included a decrease in its flexibility, a slowdown in its processing time of transactional work, and a decrease in job satisfaction among HR managers (Patel et al. 2019).

Research using data from a study of firms in Spain attends directly to this question of acceptance and credibility. The research found that the credibility of the HR function is only one of the factors that influence employees' acceptance of HR's role. Other essential elements were top management and supervisor support, and that supervisor support carries more weight than that of top managers (Stirpe et al. 2013). Similar results are reported from a study of subsidiaries of Nordic multinationals though in this instance the attitudes of the unit managers were found to be especially important (John and Bjorkman 2015).

We now turn to recent work which attends directly to the question of contemporary HR competences. Unlike the mainly UK-based studies above, the ones which follow are mainly American-based though with some global survey evidence included. The perspectives described below also tend to be more prescriptive in nature than the descriptive accounts discussed so far.

HR competences which make a difference

There have been a number of attempts to delineate HR competences: the knowledge, skills, and abilities required of HR professionals. Many HR associations, independent organizations, researchers, and consultants have worked to define the competences required for HR professionals. For example, HR has been encouraged to increase its analytical competence (Angrave et al. 2016) and to make HR 'relevant to business' (Kryscynski and Ulrich 2015).

The discussion of competences for HR professionals is an extension of the general competency-based approach to building leaders. One of the first large-scale applications of competences to the work environment occurred during World War II as the United States Army Air Corps applied competency logic in selecting and training fighter pilots. Following the war, a central figure in the Air Force's task force applied this approach to a division of General Motors. This approach was advanced by David

McClelland in 1973 in *Testing for Competences*, and further developed by Richard Boyatzis, then of the McBer and Company consulting firm, in his influential book, *The Competent Manager* (Boyatzis 1982).

The task of defining personal competences for HR professionals began across organizations in the 1970s with work by the American Society for Training and Development. This examined the competences of those involved in human resource development (McLagan and Bedrick 1983). Since then, a number of attempts have been made to define the competences required by HR professionals more widely. This included a series of surveys of HR practitioners and line managers starting in 1987 with a sample of 10,291 through to 2017 with a sample of 31,868 managers (Ulrich et al. 2017). Similar work was conducted by the Center for Effective Organizations over a 20-year period from 1996 to 2015 (Lawler and Boudreau 2009; 2012). Likewise, consultancy firms such as Boston Consulting Group and Deloitte have undertaken surveys of trends in HR which highlight emerging competences in HR. Professional societies such as the Chartered Institute of Personnel and Development (CIPD) and the Society for Human Resource Management (SHRM) have also conducted their own periodic surveys which have tracked trends and changing emphases such as the growing focus on talent management and leadership (CIPD 2022).

Ulrich et al. (2017) identified four key principles that shape choices for defining HR competences.

First, competences that create positive outcomes were identified as being central. These authors suggest that most competency models ask the question, 'What are the competences of HR professionals?', whereas the question should be 'What are the competences of HR professionals that create the greatest value?' Different HR competences have differential impacts on three outcomes: personal effectiveness of the HR professional, impact on key stakeholders, and business results.

Second, HR competences they suggest should be determined less by self-report and more by how those competences are perceived by others. HR competences should be assessed not only by the HR professional but by those who observe the HR professional. People generally judge themselves by their intent; others judge them by their behaviour, so it is important to evaluate both intent and behaviour (see Bracken et al. 2018).

Third, global or generic HR competences exist, but they also may vary by geography, industry, size of organization, level in the organization, role in the organization, gender, time in role, and so forth (Ulrich et al. 2012). In general, according to Ulrich, about 50–60% of HR competences are essential to all circumstances, 40–50% vary by setting.

Fourth, key HR competences change over time. As the environment changes, so do businesses, and so do personal competences required to be effective. Over time, every four to five years, about 30–40% of HR competences evolve to stay current.

These principles shape the definition, assessment, and application of HR competence models as illustrated below.

Illustration of the Ulrich HR competency model

To illustrate the process and approach to HR competences, we report on the seventh round of the HR competency study (Ulrich et al. 2017). In that 2017 round, data were collected from worldwide surveys rating the competences and performance of about 4,000 HR professionals from more than 1,200 organizational units.

In collaboration with regional HR partners, this study examined 123 specific items detailing what HR professionals should be, know, or do. These items were derived from focus groups by each of the 21 regional partners and from previous iterations of the research. Through factor analyses, nine competence domains were identified (see Figure 4.1). Three of these competences were identified as core drivers because they delivered on key outcomes:

- *Strategic positioner*: Able to position a business to win in its market. In the past, this competence domain was called business knowledge or acumen or strategic positioner. It has four elements: knowing the language of business (business literacy), knowing the business' strategy and how the business makes money, defining the expectations of key stakeholders (customers, suppliers, investors, and competitors) in the business niche, and anticipating shifts in the business environment and context.
- *Credible activist*: Able to build relationships of trust by having a proactive point of view. In the past, this competence was often called the trusted advisor or cultural guardian. When HR professionals are trusted, they are more likely to be 'invited to the table' of business dialogue. The activist dimension of this role implies that HR be proactive and initiate conversations to deliver trust.
- *Paradox navigator*: Able to manage tensions inherent in businesses (e.g., be both long- and short-term focused, be both top-down and bottom-up capable). By navigating paradox, HR professionals are able to help both organizations and people create the agility to respond to change.

This study also found three domains of HR competence that are organization enablers, helping position HR to deliver strategic value:

- *Culture and change champion*: Able to make change happen and manage organizational culture.

Figure 4.1 HR competency model for HR professionals.

- *Human capital curator*: Able to manage the flow of talent by developing people and leaders, driving individual performance, and building technical talent.
- *Total reward steward*: Able to manage employee well-being through financial and non-financial rewards.
- Three other delivery enablers that focused on managing the tactical or foundational elements of HR were also found in the study.
- *Technology and media integrator*: Able to use technology and social media to drive high-performing organizations.
- *Analytics designer and interpreter*: Able to use analytics to improve decision-making (Huselid 2018; Kryscynski et al. 2018).
- *Compliance manager*: Able to manage the processes related to compliance by following regulatory guidelines.

Each of these HR competences is important for the performance of HR professionals though of course there are many practitioners who do not achieve or display these competences. There are many details around this research (e.g., variation in competences by level, by geography, by length of service, by functional expertise, etc.), but the focus here is on three key findings related to the outcomes of HR competences. First, to be invited to the table to exercise influence, HR professionals need to demonstrate personal credibility. Second, HR professionals need to demonstrate the ability to serve multiple stakeholders. For internal stakeholders (employees, line managers), HR professionals require personal credibility, but to serve external stakeholders (customers and investors), HR professionals should be strategic positioners. Third, to create business value, HR professionals need to become paradox navigators. These three outcomes demonstrate the impact of the 'core driver' competences in Figure 4.1. Collectively, they help HR professionals deliver value by knowing what they should be, know, and do to affect their personal effectiveness, stakeholder outcomes, and business results.

It is interesting to see the evolution of HR competences over 30 years. Each of the seven rounds is independent, in that they represent a cross-section of HR professionals who rate themselves on competences and Associate Raters who rate them. Over the rounds, factor analyses showed an increase in the complexity of HR competences. In 1987, three domains were delineated: business knowledge, HR delivery, and management of change. In 1992, this was expanded to four domains, then five in 1997, and then ultimately nine domains in 2017. Being a competent HR professional has become increasingly complex, with some of the recent competences (analytics designer and interpreter; technology and social media integrator) reflecting how HR competences reflect general business trends. Competences for HR professionals have evolved with changing business conditions.

Across all competence domains, the seven rounds of survey from 1987 through to 2017 show that HR professionals have improved over these 30 years. The business knowledge score increased from 3.17 to 4.13, HR delivery from 3.33 to 4.02, and personal proficiency from 3.78 to 4.33. These are significant improvements in the overall competences for HR professionals. They offer a serious challenge to many of the doubts about the HR profession that have been expressed as exemplified in earlier parts of this chapter.

Competent HR departments

In workshops with business leaders, when asked the question: 'How would you divide ten points between individual talent (individual competences, workforce, people, employees, human capital) and "organization" (workplace, organization capabilities, systems, team-work, culture) and their relative impact on business results?' Answers range across the board, with some highlighting talent, others organization, and some neutral.

Ulrich and colleagues undertook research on this question with over 1,200 businesses and 32,000 people. They have determined for these businesses both the quality of both their organization and the competences of their people. They then correlated these two domains on the financial and stakeholder results of the business. While other factors (e.g., strategy, industry, operational excellence, and culture) impact results, they were able to divide the relative impact of talent and organization on business and stakeholder results. They report that organization has four times the impact of talent on business results. These are significant findings and imply an 8 to 2 distribution in the ten-point allocation exercise with executives. So, talent matters, but organization matters even more.

Organizations are social systems that enable people to learn to cooperate, develop talents, find a shared sense of purpose, and survive. By so doing, organizational performance is greater than individual productivity. Additionally, organizations take on identities of their own that outlast individual personalities. Enduring organizations sustain change that any single individual may initiate. When customers buy products or services from an organization (rather than an individual), they have long-term confidence in the sustainability of the organization. Investors who have more favourable impressions of an organization (versus individuals) give the organization a premium for its sustained financial performance as well as intangibles (strategy, brand, and operational systems).

This 'power of organization effect' extends also to the way the HR function itself is organized. Far less research has been done on what factors underpin effective HR departments than on the research reported above on defining HR's contribution and competences. Some of the original work on how to organize HR was captured in the work on being a business partner in the book *Human Resource Champions* (Ulrich 1997). That book outlined four roles within HR departments: administrative experts, employee champions, strategic partners, and change agents. These roles provided the basis for the model used by the CIPD and its work on the role of the 'business partner' (CIPD 2022). In popular form, three main organizational roles were widely discussed: shared services (doing administrative work), centres of expertise (doing technical specialist work), and business partners (doing generalist business-focused work). This three-legged model of how to organize a HR department became highly influential among practitioners (Holley 2016). After a couple of decades, there have also been attempts to offer alternative assessments and alternative modes of organizational arrangements for HR (Roebuck 2015; Scott-Jackson and Mayo 2017). The model has also attracted critique (Adams 2016).

Many of the critiques apply the 1997 business partner model to business issues 20 years later. In the ensuing 20 years, much has changed in the world of technology and much has changed in the world of HR. The business partner concept has dramatically evolved from roles and outcomes to a logic of how HR delivers value to employees, organizations, customers, investors, and communities. The transformation of HR is not just about changing roles in an HR department, but a fundamental shift in how HR conceives, organizes, and delivers work. More recent work by Ulrich and colleagues (2017) identifies nine dimensions of an effective HR department. These dimensions draw on the latest work in organization design and also come from experience working with many HR departments. The updated model is shown in Figure 4.2.

Starting from the top of the figure is the dimension of HR Reputation. Every organization creates a reputation in its marketplace, which may be called its identity or brand. This reputation shapes how stakeholders perceive and act towards the organization. An HR Department creates a reputation or identity based on what value it has

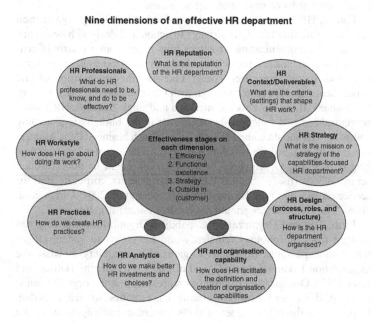

Figure 4.2 Nine dimensions of an effective HR department.

created, why HR practices are created and how they are used, and what roles HR professionals play. These reputations often outlive individual leaders and shape how others respond to the HR department.

The second dimension is HR Context/Deliverables. An organization succeeds by mastering its context and defining a unique definition of success. This definition of success sets the criteria for how the organization allocates resources and makes choices. Four sub-criteria that shape HR work have been identified: service (reduce transaction costs), create (increase technical excellence in HR practices), integrate (link HR practices to business strategy), and influence (use HR to win with customers and investors). HR departments can be focused on any or all of these four deliverables as criteria for effective work.

Third, HR Strategy. Effective organizations have a sense of direction with purpose that represents an aspiration for what can be and can include a vision of an idealized state of what the organization wants to become, a mission statement for why it exists, and strategies and goals of where and when it will invest to get there. The purpose envisions a future, sets an agenda, and offers direction. An HR department has a purpose with a mission that answers who they are (roles), what they aspire to deliver (capabilities), and why (value created). This mission focuses on results or outcomes, not activities.

Fourth, HR Design (process, roles, and structure). Every organization has a structure that translates strategy to action and deals with how work is done. These organization structures may range from a matrix of centralized (single business focused on efficiency) to decentralized (multiple businesses focused on effectiveness). Likewise, the organization of HR departments needs to match or align with the organization design logic of the business. If the business is centralized and single business, HR should be centralized and functionally organized; if the business is a holding company; HR should embed HR practices in each business; if the business is a diversified allied firm, HR would be run like a professional services firm (Ulrich and Grochowski 2012). HR work might be done through centres of expertise, embedded HR business partners, corporate staff, or service centres that may be outsourced (Lawler et al. 2004; Ulrich et al. 2008). The HR structure should match the business structure.

Fifth, HR and Organization Capability. Organization thinking has evolved from morphology (efficiency and hierarchy) to system (alignment) to capabilities (identity). Organization capability is what the organization is known for and good at doing – its identity (Ulrich and Lake 1990). Organization capabilities represent what the organization is good at doing and how it patterns its activities to deliver value. Capability is the collective set of skills, expertise, and alignment of the people in the company that create the identity of the organization both internally and externally – ultimately, what it is known for.

Sixth, HR Analytics. Information has become a central issue for analyzing organizations. Every Nobel Prize winner in economics who focuses on organization (institutions) as the unit of analysis frames organization as information (e.g., George Akerlof, Kenneth Arrow, Ronald Coase, Friedrich Hayek, Herbert Simon, Michael Spence, James Tobin, and Oliver Williamson). Likewise, over the last decade, 'analytics' has become a buzzword in HR and an increasingly important concept for HR's future. There are two major challenges to HR departments using analytics to drive stakeholder and business results. When talking about analytics, a number of concepts are used: scorecards, dashboards, predictive analytics, data science, evidence-based decisions, metrics, human resource accounting, cloud (or big) data, forecasting, or workforce modelling. The underlying agenda of all these efforts is to access and use information to make better decisions. The role of analytics has evolved in four stages: scorecards to insights to interventions to impact (Rasmussen and Ulrich 2015).

Seventh, HR Practices. An HR department is often known by the HR practices it creates and establishes throughout the organization. Four criteria for designing and delivering HR practices have been identified: innovative (based on the latest research), integrated (offering systems solutions not isolated HR practices), aligned (connected not just to strategy, but to customers and investors outside the firm), and simple (increasingly a focus on simplicity has shaped HR practices). An effective HR department has functional experts who can create HR practices around these criteria.

Eighth, HR Professionals. This is concerned with what HR professionals need to be, know, and do to deliver key outcomes. This topic was reviewed earlier in this chapter.

Ninth, HR Work Style: How does HR go about doing its work? HR practitioners, when working effectively, will make it easy for stakeholders (line managers, employees, and customers) to access HR solutions and HR techniques. The characteristics of a high-relating HR department have been defined as: share a common purpose, respect differences, govern and connect, care for one another, share experiences, and grow together.

These nine criteria for an effective HR department build upon and extend previous work on HR transformation and broaden the focus of the HR department to an overall logic. These nine criteria for an HR department may be seen as delivering value at four stages (see Figure 4.3)

Each of these waves has a focus on different HR outcomes: *Foundational/Administrative*: HR focuses on efficiency; *Functional*: HR focuses on best practices; *Strategic*: HR focuses on delivering strategy; *Outside in*: HR focuses on increasing value to stakeholders outside the organization. The nine dimensions can be arrayed against these four

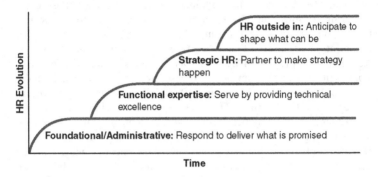

Figure 4.3 Waves of HR value creation.

outcomes which result in a matrix that can be used to describe, audit, or improve the overall effectiveness of an HR department. For example, to take the dimension 'HR Reputation', under the foundational/administrative stage would be characterized as about efficiency and the department would be known for delivering tasks efficiently and effectively. Under the functional stage, it would be known for its performance in the different functional areas. Under the strategic stage, it would be known and evaluated with respect to how its work aligned with, and supported, the business strategy. Under the outside in stage, it will be evaluated with regard to how well the function understands and responds to external stakeholders such as customers, investors, and the community. To take another example, using the dimension of 'HR Analytics', the foundational stage would use this to refer to a HR scorecard to measure the past performance of the department, at the functional stage analytics would offer insight into people and organization; at the strategic stage analytics would focus on measuring HR interventions that can be shown to contribute to the business strategy; and at the outside in stage analytics would be used to measure business impact, the HR scorecard becomes the same as the business scorecard (Ulrich et al. 2012).

Conclusion

As the chapter has shown, research on the subject of the HR function over the past few decades has produced portraits of contrasting forms. One set of accounts suggests an optimistic view with increasing evidence of enhanced capabilities and positive contributions. But other, more sceptical accounts suggest that the function has yet to attain in practice the kind of elevated status or the influence which has been outlined in conceptual models. The origins of the function are found in personnel administration and much of the early work portrayed an occupational group that lacked influence despite attempts to establish a 'professional' status. The emergence of HRM appeared to offer the opportunity, the logic, and the tools to enable a more strategic role for the function. The evidence from the studies described in the early part of the chapter tended to point towards the uncertain and even fragile standing of the function, but the latter part of the chapter offered material pointing towards a far more optimistic picture. Both depictions reflect different realities of time and place. Context matters hugely in HRM. This is the subject of the next chapter.

Acknowledgement

The authors would like to acknowledge the valuable contribution of Dave Ulrich to the writing of this chapter.

5 The changing contexts of strategic human resource management

As emphasized in the first chapter, the SHRM phenomenon (in its distinctive sense denoting a high-commitment approach) can be seen as a product of its time. It emerged and spread when international pressures were making many firms in western economies uncompetitive and new ways of working were being sought. The post-Second World War consensus was in the process of breaking down and a shift was underway that offered an alternative to conventional wisdom and practices based on managing labour through temporary truces secured through collective bargaining. At first, only a few corporations (examples included General Electric, Hewlett Packard, and Eli Lilley) led the way in installing an approach to employment that sought 'commitment' in place of mere acquiesce (Walton 1985). As noted, the new approach started from the perspective of the workforce as an 'asset' and not simply a cost; these assets merited investment in this form of capital – the human capital. For example, Jeffrey Pfeffer made the case for *Competitive Advantage through People* (Pfeffer 1994). From the late 1980s onwards, the pioneering firms were imitated by a host of more mainstream organizations in both the private and public sectors as revealed by empirical case research (Storey 1992). Initial doubts about whether HRM would be able to establish itself gave way to wider adoption.

Of course, this interpretation relates only to the *distinctive version* of HRM, as noted in the first chapter. In the wider, looser usage, employment decisions might be ad hoc, short-term, and reactive. Hence, just as in the field of strategic management itself, there are multiple meanings of 'strategy'. It can be variously a plan, a pattern, a position, a perspective, or a ploy (Mintzberg et al. 1998; Mintzberg and Lampel 1999). Low-road approaches as well as high-road approaches can be 'strategic' if decisions about employment matters (recruitment, reward, and appraisal) are not merely isolated processes but reflect and are informed by, some explicit intent that aligns employment choices to business organization choices (Storey 1992).

DOI: 10.4324/9781003364276-6

But changing contexts in recent decades have triggered and enabled changing employment practices – often of a very radical kind. Some of these changes seem to signal a reverse of the emphasis on high-commitment working and a shift to outsourcing, sub-contracting, short-term, even zero-hour contracts, precarious work, and a growing disparity in rewards. Growing income inequality in the USA has been systematically traced by two Harvard and California University economists (Lindert and Williamson 2017), while MIT economist Peter Temin (2017) likewise tracks the negative impacts of the 'dual economy'. The metaphor of the 'hourglass economy' refers to the hollowed-out middle of the labour market with a growing disparity between high and low earners (London Assembly 2016). It is reflected in a 'squeezed middle' and growing income inequality, not just wealth inequality. For most of the 20th century, the central employment relationship was between a large employer and a set of directly employed workers with relative job security and a host of employment benefits. In the past couple of decades, a wider range of employee/employer relationships have been formed. While most employees still work full-time and on 'permanent' contracts, an increasing number of others are working part-time and in a multitude of contractual relationships. Employment has often been devolved to a complex web of smaller contracting agencies that participate in equally complex supply chains. Terms and conditions which had improved in the 20th century among the large employing bureaucracies (Edwards 1979) went into reverse in this latter period. Many workers are reported as valuing flexibility and yet at the same time the picture is complex and contested because work in many organizations became less well-rewarded and more precarious (Standing 2011; Kalleberg 2013; 2018). As Kalleberg (2018) notes, there appears to be a growth, rather than a diminution, of 'bad jobs' even if these latter are not always necessarily precarious.

Some of these trends can be traced to larger, mega-trends. One such is the rise of the 'intangible economy'. This term denotes a shift from investment in tangible assets such as factories and machinery to intangible assets such as design, software, and branding (Haskel and Westlake 2018). Firms illustrating this trend include Apple, Google, and TikTok. Haskel and Westlake spell out a whole range of major and sustained consequences stemming from this shift. These include a substantial rise in inequality and shifts in power consequent to the differential ability to benefit from the exploitation of intangibles. The thesis is that investment in intangible assets carries certain characteristic features which make them distinctive from traditional tangible assets. Intangible assets tend to be more scalable (with relatively little extra investment they can be scaled up and thus come to dominate a marketplace), their costs are more likely to be sunk (they are more risky because failed assets cannot so easily be sold), they are more subject to spillovers (ideas and inventions can be used multiple times and potentially by multiple players), and they benefit disproportionately from synergies. Haskell and Westlake explore the many economic and social consequences associated with the rise of intangibles, but the human resource management implications have yet to be fully investigated. Many of the institutions and assumptions about labour relations and the management of employees which were built during the industrial era may not be so relevant under the radically different economic conditions prevailing in an intangible economy.

The implications of the intangible economy context for human resource management may play out in a variety of ways. Haskel and Westlake (2018) note how the intangibles of the operating system in Amazon warehouses constrain employees with tight monitoring and an inherent command and control regime. Conversely, organizations that *produce* intangible assets, such as software writing, design, and research and development, will probably want to foster autonomy, retain talent, and promote commitment.

The COVID-19 pandemic brought many repercussions for work and human resource management. One effect included the wholesale emergence of working from home, furlough (Huffman et al. 2022), and employment disruptions alongside apparent new assessments of the wage-effort bargain, hybrid working, and the changing nature of implicit contracts (as explored in a special issue of *Human Resource Management* Vol 61(3) 2022).

Felstead and Reuschke (2021) researched the surge in homeworking in the UK during the pandemic and assessed its impact on productivity. Putting the phenomenon in context they noted that it had taken almost 40 years for homeworking to grow by three percentage points, but it grew eightfold in 2020 because of the pandemic. Employees reported that their productivity was not adversely affected – seven out of ten employees said that they were able to get as much done while working at home in June 2020 as they were able to do six months earlier.

Furlough is an interesting HR intervention because it has so many variants and potential responses. Essentially furlough refers to a temporary lay-off. The job is kept open for a limited time, and the employee is expected to return to that job after the specified lay-off period. One version and one response may view this as an enlightened policy that keeps employment open and which retains at least some measure of compensation (potentially reaching 100% but more frequently a proportion of this). But another perspective views furlough as a type of 'cutback strategy' and finds varied reactions to potential breaches of the psychological contract (Huffman et al. 2022). Some uses of furlough or temporary lay-off in the USA appear to suggest leave without pay. Such interventions can be seen to potentially threaten trust, commitment, and perceived fairness.

A valuable resource that assesses these issues across all 27 EU countries is to be found in the report by the European Foundation for the Improvement of Living and Working Conditions (Eurofound 2022). Using a series of surveys, it tracks how lockdowns transformed labour markets, the types of state intervention to protect employment and businesses, remote working and furloughs, patterns of inequality, the fragmentation of work and employment relationships and the ways in which (against expectations) labour supply became restricted as economies recovered. The report shows that at its peak in quarter 2 of 2020, the number of workers on furlough across the 27 EU member states reached 13.8 million which was 17% of the total workforce. The report shows how job losses disproportionately hit workers on temporary contracts. A related resource on the implications of COVID-19 for work can be found in: *eurofound.link/ef20050* (accessed 1st Feb 2023). Likewise, the International Labor Organisation, a United Nations agency, reported that in 2021 around one-third of workers in the leading economies were supported by their governments on one kind or other of a furlough scheme (ILO 2021).

Contrary to expectations about the large-scale loss of jobs and hence high unemployed at the end of state-subsidized 'furloughs', the period following the lifting of restrictions saw labour shortages. In part, this was attributed to migrant workers returning to their home countries but in addition another social and economic phenomenon was said to be in play. The 'Great Resignation' is a label and an idea popularized by Anthony Klotz of Texas A&M University. Klotz noted the rise in quit rates and the degree to which employees were not returning to their workplaces in the expected manner. This includes mid-career people taking early retirement (see the 'Great Resignation' report from the World Economic Forum (2021). This phenomenon raises some interesting research questions. These include its extent and nature, its distribution across socio-economic and occupational groups, the source of alternative forms of income and, not least, the changing nature of the meaning of work, and its role in social identity and status.

A less visible form of reappraisal and withdrawal is known as 'quiet quitting'. This refers to the obverse of high commitment and can be manifested in minimal effort and engagement while nominally continuing to work at a job. Running alongside this in the post-pandemic world has been a notable increase in strikes and other forms of industrial action as workers and unions seek to at least match the increases in price inflation. In the UK, notable examples have occurred in the railways, the postal services, and in other mainly public sector organizations. Strikes and protests about the rising costs of living have also been recorded in France, Belgium, and other European countries during 2022/2023.

Developments such as those outlined above carry numerous implications for the management of human resources as traditional assumptions come under challenge and they offer enticing future research opportunities.

The ebb and flow of HRM

The post-war settlement in many of the advanced economies was based on a tri-partite employment governance system brokered by employers, trade unions, and the state. Employment relations were governed by a 'system of rules' (Dunlop 1958). The conflict was managed through the negotiation of the rules governing pay rates, holiday entitlements, and rights of representation. The rules were thus procedural and substantive. In the background, as a kind of safety net, were employment laws covering, for example, health and safety at work, child labour, and redundancy. But, in the main, the parties preferred the 'voluntarist system' based on collective bargaining rather than an 'interfering' state (Flanders 1970). In consequence, employment was governed by elaborate and detailed collective agreements negotiated at the industry sector level as well as at company level. The resulting written agreements were often lengthy and very detailed. Variations had to be subject to renegotiation.

That was the order of things for a number of decades. It was a product of the economic and social conditions prevailing at the time. Under these conditions, the prized skills of the labour manager were based on negotiation. Industrial relations specialists and trade union leaders were in high demand as were arbitrators. But that 'system' (Dunlop 1958) began to unravel as alternatives were developed which seemed to meet better the challenges of more competitive global trade. One of the main alternatives can be characterized as forming the shift to HRM.

The 'productivity agreements' of the 1970s in a sense presaged the way as flexibility was traded for pay (Flanders 1964). The HRM movement seemed to take this a significant step further. HRM specialists (in staffing, training, compensation, and organization design) began to displace industrial relations specialists as the link between employment approaches and business strategy was made more explicit. The *method* of managing labour was posited as a source of competitive advantage rather than a mere afterthought or as a given.

Entrepreneurship, finance, and ownership

But further changes in context have prompted further changes in employment practices. A key set of drivers stemmed from new forms of finance, ownership, and organizational (re)structuring. Organizations faced heighted competition in an increasingly global marketplace for services, goods, capital, and labour. There was an erosion of life-time employment, and measures were introduced to increase accountability. Agency theory (Jensen and Meckling 1976) proposed that employees were more productive when they acted as 'owners' rather than as 'agents' of others. Employees became increasingly responsible for their personal career choices. The threat of this accountability was that employees who did not meet changing work conditions were often left out; while employees with high value-added skills were given opportunities to learn and to grow. However, high-commitment working built around high skill and high wages has, in many instances, gone into reverse. In the decade 1996 to 2006, there was a 50% reduction in publicly traded firms in North America (Ulrich et al. 2017). In large part, these firms were merged with other firms, or they turned to private equity for leveraged buy-outs where employees were made more accountable for their own work. In early private equity deals, firms would focus on a 'buy and sell' strategy to strip out costs and to resell the firm as quickly as possible. The workforce was often seen as a cost to be reduced.

The epitome of this trend is captured by the concept of 'financialization' (Batt and Appelbaum 2013; Appelbaum and Batt 2014). This denotes a tendency towards an economic system where firms are treated in a new way, with less emphasis on investment and growth and more emphasis on opportunistic speculation and financial manipulation. Hedge funds and private equity firms acquire enterprises, restructure them, and load them with debt before selling them. This results in firms becoming more unstable and, in consequence, labour once again is regarded as an afterthought.

But in some recent analyses of private equity, it has been suggested that employees and leadership are seen as a valued asset to be nurtured and developed. In leading private equity firms, leadership capital partners are figuring out how to define and invest in leadership, talent, and culture to increase the value of the firm (Ulrich and Allen 2017). These 'buy and build' approaches link HR issues to sustainable shareholder value. The implication of more transparent financial accountability is that employees who lack skills may be downsized, delayered, or outsourced, but the opportunities for employees who are agents for their development are higher. HR plays a paradoxical role in these settings. On the one hand, HR policies demand that all employees are treated equally and with respect, but on the other, HR responds to market pressures by requiring differentiation of employees based on performance.

The diverse ways of raising finance for business carry implications for the management of human resources. Seed funding, angel investors, private equity and public, management buy-outs, venture capital, peer-to-peer lending, crowd funding, or employee ownership each brings shades of influence on the conduct of business. One aspect is that many of these involve active investors who seek to directly influence management. Di Pietro et al. (2022) explore different kinds of entrepreneurial financing and their implications for HR practices. They provide a framework of different 'investor logics' along with different investment time horizons to unpick operational, strategic, and transformational HRM practices identified in their sample companies. For example, they found that firms in the early stages of growth that receive funding from angel investors or bank equity tended to adopt an operational approach to their human resource management practices. Kuvandikov et al. (2022) find that activist hedge funds tend to be associated with workforce reduction and with no clear gains in labour productivity.

The key point is that the source and nature of finance can crucially affect the nature of the human resource policies and practices adopted. Despite some interesting contributions, such as the Special Issue of the *British Journal of Management* devoted to the theme of entrepreneurial finance (Budhwar et al. 2022), this remains rich, promising and as yet still relatively under-researched terrain for HR scholars.

The gig economy

In recent years, the 'gig economy' (Graham et al. 2017), as epitomized by Uber, has come to characterize trends in the nature of modern work even though it is as yet a statistically small part of the employed population. Graphic descriptions of the experience of work in the low-wage zero-hours economy can be found in James Bloodworth's book, *Hired: Six Months Undercover in Low Wage Britain* (Bloodworth 2018).

A measured and research-based analysis of the nature and size of the more precarious forms of work can be found in *The Rise of Alternative Work Arrangements in the United States 1995–2015* (Katz and Krueger 2016). They report that alternative forms of work (contracting, sub-contracting, on-call workers, freelancers, agency staff, etc.) are growing faster than conventional employment opportunities. These peripheral forms of work increased overall from 10.1% of the US workforce in 2005 to 15.8% in 2015. More starkly, the growth in this form of work accounted for over 90% of net new employment amounting in total to 23.6 million American workers by November 2015. According to *Forbes Magazine* by 2021, the 'gig economy' in the USA accounted for 35% of the workforce (Zgola 2021).

One consequence of the growth of these kinds of work has been the decline in the share of GDP going to labour across a number of different countries (Karabarbounis and Neiman 2013; Piketty 2014). In *The Fall of the Labor Share and the Rise of Superstar Firms*, Autor et al. (2017) note the decline in the labour share of rewards compared with capital over the decade up to 2014 in the large countries that account for two-thirds of world GDP.

While some of these work contracting arrangements give employees the flexibility and autonomy they desire, the downside is that many of these alternative work arrangements offer lower financial and health care benefits. So, the optimism of the early HRM movement has given way, to a large extent, to a more pessimistic assessment of deteriorating conditions of work and employment for many people. This is epitomized in David Weil's book about the 'fissured workplace' (Weil 2014). Weil, a former adviser to President Obama, argues that fissuring represents a fragmentation of the traditional corporation. It comes in the forms of franchising and outsourcing. One example he offers is Hyatt Regency Hotels in Boston which fired longstanding full-time staff and replaced them with outsourced agency staff at a much lower rate and without benefits (echoed, as noted earlier, by P&O Ferries in 2022). Weil sees a profound shift that has not been fully recognized. He sees it as spreading way beyond its traditional confines such as construction and cleaning services spreading both vertically in terms of occupations, and horizontally across sectors. The fissured workplace may contain multiple re-combinations of contracting organizations. Far from identifying with and being committed to their employing organizations, some workers are not even sure who actually employs them or if they are employed or not. Thus, 'under the hood' of the main brand there can be multiple subcontracted service organizations.

Such trends raise the question as to the part played by human resource managers. Is their advice side-lined or are they central architects and operational agents of the new forms? The dynamics of this offers a promising subject for future research.

Regulation and public policy initiatives

Public policy and labour law have been behind the curve in relation to the developments in new forms of work. In Canada, the Ministry of Labour for Ontario commissioned a *Changing Workplaces Review* to respond to the secular shift to precarious work. This stemmed from a concern that existing labour laws were not adequate for dealing with the new fragmented and precarious employment landscape (Mitchell and Murray 2017). The UK government set up a similar review led by Matthew Taylor, a former adviser to Prime Minister Tony Blair. This commission produced a report entitled *Good Work: The Taylor Review of Modern Working Practices* (Taylor 2018). Both reports offered tentative suggestions pointing to the need to approach new forms of regulation with some caution. The response so far from the UK government has been to suggest consultation on a possible series of regulatory measures including all new staff to be given, on their first day at work, a list of their rights including holiday and sick pay entitlement, a right to a payslip for all workers including casual and zero-hour workers, and a requirement for agency workers to be informed who pays them and for clarity on all deductions from wages.

Referring to trends in the USA, Weil noted:

> Many of the industries where researchers in recent years have found high rates of violations of basic labour standards and worsening employment conditions coincide with industries where fissuring is most advanced. These include restaurant and hospitality sectors, janitorial services, many segments of manufacturing, residential construction, and home health care.
>
> (Weil 2014)

He also notes however that fissuring has now become prevalent across many sectors of the economy.

Labour laws designed to protect workers often have company-size threshold and these are easily by-passed when sub-contracting occurs. In the introduction to a symposium on work in the 'gig economy' published in *The Economic and Labour Relations Review* (2017), it is noted that theoretical and empirical research into this phenomenon is 'in its infancy'. Uber and Deliveroo exemplify the platform-based businesses of the gig economy. Once again, the uncertainties about how to respond to the phenomenon are emphasized. It is noted that 'While digital platform work shares powerful continuities with much older work formations, it also presents modern policymakers and trade unions with a variety of new political, regulatory, and legal challenges' (Flanagan 2017, p. 378). One interpretation suggests that these forms of casualised work are not new and that they represent reincarnations of age-old attempts to allow access to work on an unrestricted basis (Stanford 2017). There is the possibility that digitization will permit and impel the wider diffusion of this business model and hollow out more extensively the standard employment model. There is often an implied inevitability about this technology-driven trend, but others are intent on countering this determinism by pointing to the wider range of economic and regulatory forces to set alongside the technological (Stanford 2017).

Arguably, the trends described are more characteristic of Anglo-American contexts but less so of many other economies. A distinction has been drawn between stock-exchange-focused financing, which is especially characteristic of many firms in Anglo-Saxon countries, and other means of raising capital, which is typical of firms in countries such as Japan, Germany, and Italy. The former approach has been linked to short-termism in behaviour as companies need to report quarterly to shareholder representatives who normally seek evidence of profitable returns. Failure to produce results may mean sale of the stocks and a fall in the stock price and thus the value of the enterprise. In contrast, firms which raise capital in other ways – perhaps through close relations with regional banks – are more able to focus on the longer term and can thus invest in resources such as machinery and training which cost money in the short-term but can deliver profits over the longer term. A similar point can be made in relation to employee-owned companies (Salaman and Storey 2016).

In their examination of these variations, Hall and Soskice use the term 'varieties of capitalism' (Hall and Soskice 2001). According to these analysts, institutions (such as joint stock companies, investment banks, educational bodies, and stock markets) are shaped not only by laws but by informal rules or common knowledge acquired by actors through history and culture. 'Institutional complementarities' theory suggests that nations with particular types of institutions in, say, the economics sphere, develop complementary institutions in other spheres. This could include a supporting system of laws and conventions and ways of behaving.

Hall and Soskice argue that there are two main types of market economies. The first type is made up of the 'liberal market economies' (LMEs) such as the USA, the UK, Canada, and Australia; the second type includes the 'coordinated market economies' (CMEs) such as Germany, Japan, and Sweden. Hall and Soskice argue that the institutional arrangements of a nation's political economy tend to push its firms toward particular kinds of business strategy. These strategies are associated with different approaches to the hiring and firing of workers, to degrees of investment in training, and to employment security. This means, in turn, that HRM can be significantly different within and across these contrasting types of institutional contexts.

Drivers of change: globalization and technology

Globalization has not only made the world 'shrink' but has changed how and where people work. This has meant that many firms are now global organizations. Importantly, firms often expand beyond their original national borders to increase profit. This can be based on wanting to exploit an emerging market or to take advantage of new resources. Such expansion often allows them to better compete in an increasingly international market wherein few firms are 'safe'.

The ways in which globalization is playing out in the sphere of human resource management have been and are being intensively studied. The interplay between competition, cost, technologies, and local contexts is central to such analyses. The following quotation sums up a central thesis,

> Because countries have different institutional legacies or 'starting points', and different industrial relations systems, they vary in their ability to absorb new work practices from abroad; and even where they do absorb these practices, they transform them in the process. Lean production, for example, has quite different characteristics in Denmark, the United Kingdom, and Japan.
>
> (Batt et al. 2009, p. 457)

Multinational corporations present some of the greatest challenges to those working within HRM. Working across different international contexts with diverse and potentially conflicting cultural understandings and practices can be difficult. It requires considerable skill. One way to manage the challenge is through the effective transfer of knowledge within and between organizations. This requires the creation of appropriate HRM strategies.

One question is the extent to which different national settings produce and sustain distinctive practices and the challenge which these may present to HR managers who have to decide whether to seek to standardize or to work with continued variety and to adapt to local circumstances. This is important for any organisation which is seeking to do business outside its 'home' country environment – especially if it wishes to directly employ people in these different countries.

Another (wider) question is the extent to which the differences are found across borders are tending towards a reduced importance because of a 'convergence' of practices or whether varied practices will remain divergent.

With regard to technology, the automation of routine tasks has devalued traditional unskilled labour. As technology develops in the form of artificial intelligence (AI), middle-class occupations and professions face a similar deskilling. Examples include radiography and some aspects of legal work. At the same time, digitalization has enabled and reduced the costs of coordination of tasks and this has allowed the growth of outsourcing and the management of complex supply chains and networks (Tsay et al. 2018). Examples here include the falling costs of tracking goods as they are delivered from online order to home or workplace delivery. This surveillance capability intertwines with the fragmentation of the delivery workforce using such arrangements as subcontracting and self-employment.

A number of studies have reported from the front line of digitalization. A critical assessment of the changing nature and intensification of work in Amazon warehouses can be found in the book *The Warehouse: Workers and Robots at Amazon* (Delfanti 2021). This work was based on interviews conducted between 2017 and 2021 mainly in Italy and to a lesser extent in other countries. It details the nature of digital surveillance and the regimes of control of workers. A rather different perspective on the same company is presented by Bryar and Carr (2022) in their book, *Working Backwards: Insights, Stories, and Secrets from Inside Amazon.* This latter work is written by two former Amazon executives and it presents a distillation of what they see as the key lessons about the leadership and management methods deployed by Amazon. Likewise, another former executive of Amazon sets out the 14 leadership principles which he claims as at the core of that company's growth (Rossman 2021).

With regard to the question of the contribution of Artificial Intelligence (and humanoid robot versions in particular) to productivity, research by Giudice et al. (2022) suggests that such technology has so far not directly impacted labour productivity but they find some indirect impact through revised routines.

Digitalization and the rise of the internet are transforming the nature of work. New skills are required, new methods of recruiting and selecting employees are happening, and new policies are required to govern how and for what purposes digital communication may be used in work time (and the very notion of what 'work time' means today is opened up for debate as exemplified by work undertaken during commuting time and time allocation when working from home). Advances in workforce analytics are transforming approaches to people management (Huselid 2018). Innovations such as 3D printing enable the distributed production of items with consequences for the architecture of work organizations.

With fast-changing technologies and with the spread of knowledge work there has been much interest in the appropriate form of HRM for such work settings (McIver et al. 2013). Knowledge-intensive firms, it has been argued, emphasize the need for a more sophisticated use of selection methods, a greater care to offer challenging work, and congenial work environments along with opportunities for development.

Green HRM

With so much emphasis on climate change and a growing concern about the environment more generally, it is perhaps not surprising that there has been increased attention to the role of HRM in these regards – for example, Paulet et al. (2021); Luu (2021); Ren et al. (2022); Ali (2022). One meta-review suggests that Green HRM research papers increased fivefold between 2016 and 2020 (Paulet et al. 2021).

The idea that 'Green HRM' policies and practices could potentially be key drivers of green behaviour is a crucial underpinning to much of this research as is the assessment of compliance with environmental sustainability priorities. The wider external context contains many prompts for action on the environmental challenge – for example, pressure groups and consumer concerns, investors with environmental social and governance

(ESG) concerns, government regulations, and global mobilizations as expressed in the United Nations Global Compact – see https://www. unglobalcompact.org (accessed 2nd Feb 2023).

Various aspects have been studied in recent HRM literature, including examination of the relationship between green management policies and green values of employees (Dumont et al. 2019; Alzgool 2019). Aspects of recruitment, employer/employee fit, training, retention, and job satisfaction have all been explored (Pham and Paille 2019). Economic challenges post-pandemic may pause the focus on Green HRM but the scope for future research on this topic seems evident.

Conclusions

In the light of the trends and mega-trends described above, the question arises as to how much scope for manoeuvre do HRM strategists really have? The concept of strategy implies that there are *choices* to be made. These choices may be made after conscientious and careful study, or they may occur after only cursory and superficial review of options. As we saw in the first chapter of this book, choices about HR management might be carefully constructed in a proactive manner and with longer-term goals in mind, or in an *ad hoc* manner as a reaction to events, but either way, some scope for choice is implied.

One way of approaching this question of room for manoeuvre is to look at data on the role of HR professionals over time. As reported in the previous chapter, longitudinal research by Ulrich and colleagues traced the changing competences of HR professionals. The data sets came not only from self-reports but also from external raters. From 1997 to 2017, they found that being a competent HR professional has become increasingly complex, with some of the recent competencies (analytics designer and interpreter; technology and social media integrator) reflecting how HR competencies reflect general business trends. Competencies for HR professionals have evolved with changing business conditions (Ulrich et al. 2017). This research data suggests that HR has not merely been a spectator to changing economic conditions but an active player. On the other hand, arguably, in many cases, strategic choices are made within constraining and limiting 'boundary conditions' (Paauwe and Farndale 2017). Thus, context matters greatly. A key part of the contemporary context is volatility, complexity, and uncertainty. These conditions seem to require *agility* from strategic HRM practitioners. This is the focal subject of the next chapter.

6 Fit, flexibility, and agility

As the terrain of competition for organizations becomes more global, companies must build their workforces to be able to compete in a constantly changing environment. Wright et al. (2018) identified four trends that present challenges to firms in their attempts to manage human resources. First, the increasing *pace of change* in the external environment. Second, the increasing *globalization* of firms and markets due to both increased telecommunications capability and the globalization of supply chains has resulted in firms having to manage employees across borders, each of which may have unique cultural, competitive, and regulatory constraints. Third, the increasing *importance of talent* as a competitive necessity (Chambers et al. 1998). Fourth, these trends have created a challenge in the increasing *skills gaps* in labour markets. Technology has increased skill requirements in some jobs while eliminating many lower-skilled jobs.

These trends existed prior to the COVID-19 pandemic, and that pandemic caused even greater disruptions to organizations and work (McKinsey Global Survey, 2020). Within a few days, companies had to send significant portions of their workforce out of the workplace to work from home while adjusting work processes and the work environment to provide safety to those who needed to stay in the workplace. Then, as the pandemic subsided, companies faced the need to adjust work to provide flexibility to accommodate those employees who wanted to remain working from home for at least some of the time – and to align diverse work patterns with organizational needs.

Taken together, these trends have created a situation where firms must be as efficient or even more efficient than the competitors in their current operations, while also being able to transform their products, operations, and workforce to meet new competitive challenges. That is, they require both fit and flexibility/agility. As seen in earlier chapters, these concepts are fundamental to the very idea of strategic human resource management. Hence, in this chapter, we examine in more detail

DOI: 10.4324/9781003364276-7

the conceptual/theoretical models and research regarding how firms seek to achieve *both* fit and flexibility in their HR systems.

Research papers that explore the nature of *ambidexterity* in relation to HRM often straddle the fit and flexibility boundary. A Special Edition of the US journal *Human Resource Management* (2015 vol 54 S1) featured a collection of papers that illustrate work in this area. One key example of the use of the concept is the ability of an organization to simultaneously exploit existing capabilities and resources while also exploring new ones (often referred to as exploitation *and* exploration). Different factors have been identified as contributing to this capability including, for example, organizational structural arrangements, training, employee character-istics, culture, and leadership (e.g. Junni et al. 2015).

To start the analysis of ambidexterity, fit, and flexibility, we go back to one of the definitions of SHRM discussed in the first chapter of this book. There it was defined as *'the pattern* of planned human resource deploy-ments and activities intended to enable an organization to achieve its goals' (Wright and McMahan 1992, p. 298, emphasis added). It was fur-ther noted that the major subjects within the field included 'the determi-nants of decisions about human resource practices, the composition of the human capital resource pools (skills and abilities), the specification of required human resource behaviours, and the effectiveness of these deci-sions given various business strategies and/or competitive situations' (p. 298–299). This definition sets forth the major variables to be managed. Fit derives from the statement that one focus of SHRM is to understand the effectiveness of the HR decisions *given* various business strategies, i.e., how to achieve a fit between aspects of the HR system and business strategy. As we will later see, flexibility is encompassed in the idea that the effectiveness of different decisions will depend on the competitive en-vironment, in particular, the extent to which that environment is volatile, uncertain, complex, and ambiguous (VUCA). The chapter is divided into two parts: the first part examines fit and the second turns to an ex-amination of flexibility and agility.

The concept of fit in SHRM

Many authors discuss 'fit', 'alignment', and 'congruence' as desirable characteristics, but very seldom are clear definitions of these terms of-fered. SHRM theory normally suggests that the aim should be to ensure a 'vertical' fit (with business strategy) and a 'horizontal' fit (among the various HR practices themselves). In their exploration of fit, Wright and McMahan (1992) drew upon Venkatraman's (1989) delineation of the six models of fit.

Venkatraman was concerned that the much-used notion of fit was not matched by precision in its various uses and their associated empirical tests.

To help correct this, he delineated six types. These were fit as moderation, mediation, matching, gestalts, profile deviation, and covariation. He then set out the appropriate empirical analyses for the testing of each. The first three models anchor the concept of fit to a particular criterion such as performance or effectiveness. Fit as *moderation* is characterized when it is argued that the relationship between one variable (e.g., a high-performance work system) and another variable (e.g., financial performance) depends on a third variable (e.g., type of strategy). Fit as *mediation* exists when the impact of one variable (e.g., HR practices) on another variable (e.g., performance) is through the first variable's impact on an intermediate variable (e.g., employee behaviour). Fit as *profile deviation* (degree of adherence to an externally specified profile, such as a specific configuration of HR practices that will best position a firm within its competitive environment, thus resulting in optimal performance).

The next three conceptualizations of fit are not tied to a specific criterion. Fit as *matching* suggests a match between two related variables (e.g., differentiation strategy and HPWS), but does so without regard to a criterion. Fit as *gestalts* describes the specification of specific clusters of entities that are similar in their use of multiple variables, such as identifying sets of companies, where each set of companies uses a similar profile of HR practices. One observes this view of fit in SHRM when researchers use cluster analysis to identify sets of firms that have similar sets of HR practices. Finally, fit as *covariation* entails observing a set of variables that tend to work in a pattern. This is observed in SHRM research when researchers conduct factor analyses to determine which practices tend to be used together.

In order to explore further the research on fit within the domain of SHRM, we will examine how each of Venkatraman's (1989) conceptualizations of fit has been utilized.

Fit as moderation is the most utilized. Early SHRM researchers focused on aligning HR practices with strategy and so they often examined how the relationship between HR practices and performance might differ across strategies. For instance, Huselid (1995) examined the interaction between strategies and his two HPWS scales but found no significant relationships. He also utilized this conceptualization to explore the fit between these scales and the strategic HRM index and again found no significant relationship. Finally, he examined the interaction between the two scales and found that while the regression weight was significant, the interaction term did not add significant incremental variance explained.

Delery and Doty (1996) also conducted a multi-fit approach in their study. They sought to test universalistic, contingency, and configurational models to determine which represented their data best. Because contingency models represent the fit as moderation conceptualization

(Venkatraman 1989), they examined the interaction between strategy and HR practices for each of their seven HR practices and found no significant incremental variance explained in either of their performance measures. This suggested the failure to find any support for the fit as moderation model.

The dual alignment of horizontal and vertical fit was examined by Han et al. (2019). They used market entry timing as the operationalization of strategy and also examined horizontal fit as the extent to which each of the components (ability, motivation, and opportunity) of the HPWS were implemented with similar intensities. They found that HPWS was most strongly related to performance among firms following a fast-follower strategy, followed by those who were first-movers and last those following a fence-sitter strategy, and that those effects were accentuated to the extent their HPWS displayed horizontal fit.

The internal/horizontal fit among the HPWS practice components of ability-, motivation-, and opportunity-enhancing practices at the individual level of analysis has been explored by Chung and Pak (2021). They found that each of the three components was positively related to individual performance. Regarding internal fit, they found that ability-enhancing practices had a positive effect when motivation-enhancing practices were low but not high, that similarly, opportunity-enhancing practices were positively related only when motivation-enhancing practices were low but not high, and that ability-enhancing practices were positively related when opportunity-enhancing practices were high but not low.

MacDuffie (1995) expanded on the view of fit as moderation, to consider the fit to be more than just two variables. He explored the interactions among the use of buffers in the production system, the work system, and the HR practices in predicting the productivity of automobile assembly plants. He found that this three-way interaction explained significant incremental variance supporting this broader view of fit as moderation.

Similar to Huselid's (1995) testing for fit between his two HPWS sub-scales, Su et al. (2018) examined the use of commitment- and control-based HR practices. Hypothesizing that both types of practices were necessary for optimal performance, they computed the interaction between these two sub-scales and found that the interaction did, in fact, explain significant incremental variance in performance.

Chadwick et al. (2013) also tested fit as moderation looking at organization size as a moderator of the relationship between HPWS and performance. They theorized that implementing and maintaining HPWS requires managerial attention and that larger organizations would have a larger amount of managerial attention than smaller organizations. They found support such that the relationship between HPWS and performance was greater for large relative to small organizations.

Fit in relation to external context is also a matter of interest. Gahan et al. (2019) explored the fit between HPWS and change in the environment in the determination of innovation outcomes. Using a sample from Australia they found that HPWS had a stronger relationship with innovation outcomes in stable rather than dynamic environments.

Fit as mediation is probably the most frequently and thoroughly researched model of fit. An early conceptual depiction of this model was the 'Behavioural Perspective' (Schuler and Jackson 1987), which posited that HRM systems impact performance by promoting appropriate behaviours. Schuler et al. (2001) expanded this to the four-task model stating that HRM systems function primarily to (a) identify needed employee behaviours, (b) ensure employees have necessary competencies, (c) motivate employees to exhibit the needed behaviours, and (d) provide opportunities for employees to perform successfully.

As discussed in Chapter 2 in relation to HR and performance, numerous studies have examined potential mediators between HR practices and performance. Rather than repeat our account of that literature here, we simply want to note that this conceptualization of fit has also been broadened in order to include human capital. For instance, Delery and Shaw (2001), Becker and Huselid (2006), and Lepak et al. (2006) argued that the role of HR systems is to focus on building the skills and abilities and motivating strategically relevant employees. In addition, Beltran-Martin et al. (2021) found that HR flexibility (as will be discussed below) mediated the relationship between HPWS and firm performance.

Fit as profile deviation in this area of research was best exemplified by Delery and Doty's (1996) use of a 'configurational' approach to SHRM. They identified market-oriented, internal, and middle-of-the-road configurations of employment systems, and then examined how the extent to which firms deviated from their designated profile related to performance. However, they failed to find any support for this model of fit.

One must recognize that what most commentators refer to as a 'best practice' approach to HR practices (i.e., the HPWS) is, in fact, essentially a configurational approach. It encompasses multiple variables (i.e., practices), hence it fits Venkatraman's (1989) conceptualization of profile deviation. When researchers use an index of the HPWS, they are, in fact, implicitly assuming that use of all the HPWS elements is an ideal profile, and the extent to which firms deviate from that profile negatively impacts their performance.

Fit as gestalts is best exemplified by studies that seek to group similar organizations together based on the HR practices they use. Arthur's (1992) study provided a perfect example. He surveyed the use of a number of HR practices in steel mini-mills. He then submitted the data to cluster analysis to identify clusters of mini-mills similar in their employment systems. His analysis originally identified six clusters, but he then collapsed the six into two: commitment and control approaches. Another example is Hauff et al.'s (2014) study of HRM systems in Germany. Building on Arthur's (1994) commitment and control approaches, they discovered two additional hybrid clusters: long-term oriented control and regulated commitment systems.

Fit as gestalts has also been a popular approach to examining HRM differences across nations. For instance, Ignjatovic and Svetlik (2003) used the Cran-Net data to identify countries similar in their approach to HRM. They identified four clusters which they termed 'Central Southern' (Germany, Austria, Spain, Czech Republic, Slovenia, Italy, and Portugal), 'Peripheral' (Bulgaria, Estonia, Greece, Cyprus, Ireland, Northern Ireland, and Turkey), 'Nordic' (Denmark, Finland, Norway, and Sweden), and 'Western' (UK, Switzerland, Belgium, the Netherlands, and France).

Fit as 'matching' in SHRM was first popularized with some early conceptual models of the determinants of HR practices. For instance, Lengnick-Hall and Lengnick-Hall (1988) identified the types of HR systems that would be associated with productivity, expansion, development, and redirection strategies. Similarly, Baird and Meshoulam (1988) linked the types of HR systems that would be associated with firms at different stages of their life cycles. These were all conceptual approaches to fit as matching.

However, the previously discussed work by Arthur (1992) also used a 'fit as matching' approach. After creating the commitment and control groups of companies, he then showed that mills using more of a differentiation strategy were more likely to use commitment systems and firms using more of a cost strategy were more likely to use control systems.

In a unique approach to fit as matching, Lepak and Snell (1999) developed the 'HR architecture' approach. Rather than match HR systems to strategy, they proposed a typology of different talent pools based on two dimensions: uniqueness of the skills and strategic value of the skills. They suggested that different HR systems best match talent pools within the different quadrants of their framework. In a follow-up empirical study, Lepak and Snell (2002) found support for the idea that different HRM systems match different types of talent pools.

Fit as covariation is an often used approach in the social sciences as a means of data reduction. When multiple-item scales are developed, researchers often submit the data for factor analysis. Factor analysis explores the covariation among items within the larger scale, finding 'factors' comprised of items that tend to covary more with one another than they do with the rest of the items. For instance, Huselid (1995) submitted his data to a factor analysis, revealing two factors, 'employee skills and organizational structures' and 'employee motivation', using a covariation view of fit. Similarly, Beltrán-Martín et al. (2008) specifically state 'we operationalize HPWS internal fit as covariation ... [a]ccording to this perspective the common variation of HPWS dimensions is explained by a latent factor (HPWS) that captures their covariance' (p. 1020).

The results of research on fit in SHRM have been equivocal. In particular, regarding the 'fit as moderation' model, there has been very little support and when support has been shown, it has not been replicated. There is substantial research support for the 'fit as mediation' approach, albeit that there are multiple mediators that have been demonstrated, and no consensus as to which are the most critical. The 'fit as profile deviation' has seen substantial research attention, but has seldom been shown to be related to performance. 'Fit as gestalts' has been consistently demonstrated in the SHRM and international HRM literatures, but these gestalts have not necessarily been consistent (in SHRM) or tied to outcomes. 'Fit as matching' was used early in this literature, but has been relatively ignored over the past 15 years. Finally, 'fit as covariation' has consistently been used as factor analyses are conducted and/or coefficient alphas computed on the HR practice measures in almost every study.

However, we turn our attention to the 'fit as moderation' model, because this is what most people think of when they think of fit. The failure to find this type of fit is probably attributable to the failure to adequately measure HR practices with sufficient specificity. Becker and Gerhart (1996) proposed that the architecture of HR practices consisted of multiple levels: Philosophy (overall approach to managing people), Principles (basic guidelines for how they should be managed), Policies, and Practices. Wright and Sherman (1999) noted that there might be one more level better suited to assessing fit: Products. Products refer to the outcomes that the HR practice is aimed at eliciting. Most of the research in this area has used a rather generic best practice HR measure such as the number of hours training, the use of pay for performance, etc. However, these authors suggested that if these are best practices, they would likely be used equally across different strategies, but the products that they seek to elicit would differ. For example, a firm focused on customer service might devote 20 hours of training to customer service behaviour, while one focused on cost/efficiency might devote 20 hours to process redesign skills. Similarly, the customer service organization might tie pay to customer service performance, while the cost/efficiency firm might tie pay to cost control or reduction. Thus, where firms actually try to support their strategies through HR comes not from the use of different practices, but rather from the use of the same practices *to elicit different behaviours or outcomes*.

Flexibility and agility

Virtually all of the research exploring fit has been conducted in a cross-sectional format, exploring the fit between HR practices and strategy at fixed points in time. However, the increasingly volatile nature of the competitive environment requires that organizations not only achieve fit with the conditions at the current point in time but also develop capabilities that can adapt to be able to achieve fit under a new set of competitive challenges: i.e., *adaptive capacity*. This leads to a discussion on flexibility and agility in SHRM and their role in supporting 'dynamic capabilities' (Teece et al. 1997).

Flexibility can be defined as 'a firm's abilities to respond to various demands from dynamic competitive environments', (Sanchez 1995, p. 138). Weick (1979) noted that to be flexible, firms must be able to detect changes in the environment while retaining a pool of novel actions to accommodate those changes. Teece et al. (1997) argued that firms in dynamic environments must be able to 'reconfigure the firm's asset structure, and to accomplish the necessary internal and external transformation' (p. 520). Thus, in their framework, high-flexibility firms possess the capability to 'scan the environment, evaluate markets and competitors, and to quickly accomplish reconfiguration and transformation ahead of competition' (p. 520).

Related to the concept of flexibility is the more recent construct of 'organizational ambidexterity' (OA). OA has been described as the ability of a firm to simultaneously pursue efficient capitalization on current opportunities while innovating to meet the needs of future markets (Andriopoulos and Lewis 2009; Benner and Tushman 2003; Gibson and Birkinshaw 2004). Within this literature, people have referred to the ability to exploit existing competencies while exploring, through innovation, the next generation of products and services necessary to enhance future competitiveness (Abernathy 1978; Brown and Eisenhardt 1998; Levinthal and March 1993). Birkinshaw and Gibson (2004) defined 'alignment' as 'a clear sense of how value is being created in the short term and how activities should be coordinated and streamlined to deliver value' (p. 47), and defined 'adaptation' as a firm's 'ability to move quickly toward new opportunities, to adjust to volatile markets, and to avoid complacency' (p. 1). Each of these discussions of ambidexterity coincides clearly with our approach to flexibility.

Milliman et al. (1991) noted two views of the relationship between fit and flexibility in the strategic HRM literature. The 'orthogonal' perspective suggests that fit and flexibility serve as opposite ends of the same spectrum. The 'complementary' perspective argues that fit and flexibility are independent of one another, and both are essential to effective functioning of organizations. Wright and Snell (1998) took the complementary perspective and proposed that fit 'as a state that exists at some point in time ... it can only be assessed as a snapshot: fit at time 1 in no way guarantees fit at time 2' (p. 757). Flexibility, on the other hand, represents a characteristic or a trait signifying an ability to meet changing competitive needs. Thus, they argued that while it might be assessed as a trait at one point in time, 'confirmatory evidence that flexibility existed at time 1 is best examined by observing a successful adaptation to an environmental change at time 2' (pp. 757–758).

In order to explore flexibility in SHRM, it is important to note that the major model is built upon Sanchez's (1995) analysis. He proposed two types of flexibility. 'Resource flexibility' describes the range of alternative uses to which a resource can be applied, the cost and difficulty of switching to an alternative use, and the time required to do so. 'Coordination flexibility' refers to how well a firm can resynthesize strategy, reconfigure resources, and redeploy those resources. Using this as a foundation, Wright and Snell (1998) noted how both resource and coordination flexibility might be exemplified with regard to HRM practices, human capital skills, and employee behaviours. This model has driven much of the HR flexibility research.

For example, Bhattacharya et al. (2005) relied on the ideas of Wright and Snell to develop a measure of HR flexibility. They generated a list of items based on an extensive literature review and discussions with managers, and then modified the items based on input from HR managers and scholars. Their 50-item measure was then administered to 117 HR executives, and factor analysis revealed a 22-item measure consisting of three factors: HR practice flexibility, skill flexibility, and behaviour flexibility. Each of these factors was shown to be related to objective measures of firm financial performance in a cross-sectional study.

Ketkar and Sett (2009) added the construct of 'flexibility inducing' HR practices to the literature on HR flexibility. They began with Bhattacharya's measures of skill, behaviour, and HR practice flexibility, but also developed a 22-item measure of practices that induce flexibility (e.g., 'We use selection methods that help us to detect employee flexibility and adaptability'). In a cross-sectional study of Indian organizations, they found that flexibility-inducing HR practices were related to skill, behaviour, and HR practice flexibility. They also found that their flexibility measures were related to employee, operational, and financial performance. However, because all measures came from the same respondent, it is difficult to conclude any causal relationships. Using the same data set, Ketkar and Sett (2010) also showed that managers' perceptions of the environmental dynamism was related to HR flexibility.

Ngo and Loi (2008) examined the relationship between HR flexibility and adaptability culture. Collecting data from HR directors/managers in multinational companies in Hong Kong, they used shortened versions of

Bhattacharya et al.'s (2005) HR practice, skill, and behaviour flexibility. They found that employee behaviour flexibility and HR practice flexibility were both related to adaptability culture, but that skill flexibility was not, and that adaptability culture was related to both HR-related and market-related performance measures.

Given the pace of change in competitive environments, Beltrán-Martin et al. (2008) suggested that HR flexibility might mediate the relationship between HPWS and performance. Unlike previous studies that included HR practices flexibility, they operationalized HR flexibility with a scale containing items regarding functional flexibility, skill malleability, and behavioural flexibility. Their data suggested that HPWS was related to performance, but that when the mediating effect of HR flexibility was accounted for, the HPWS effect became non-significant, suggesting that HR flexibility was the mechanism through which HPWS impacted performance.

Taking this idea of flexibility further, Chang et al. (2013) explored what they termed 'flexibility-oriented HRM systems' (FHRM) and their relationship with absorptive capacity and firm innovativeness. They distinguished FHRM from HR flexibility, defining it as 'a set of internally consistent HRM practices that enable a firm to acquire and develop human resources for a wide range of alternative uses and to redeploy those resources quickly and effectively' (p. 1926). In a sample of Chinese high-tech firms, they found that both components of FHRM (coordination FHRM and resource FHRM) were related to the potential for absorptive capacity, but that only coordination FHRM was related to realized absorptive capacity. They also found that absorptive capacity was related to firm innovativeness and market responsiveness.

Patel et al. (2013) argued that as opposed to purely structural approaches to building flexibility/ambidexterity, the skills, and decisions of the human capital pool play a key role. They suggested that 'one set of HR activities helps to build a resource base capable of exploiting existing market realities, while another set of activities works to simultaneously build the resource adaptability necessary to exploit new opportunities' (p. 1423). They then hypothesized and found support for the fact that HPWS were related to OA and that OA partially mediated the relationship between HPWS and firm growth.

Note that these studies, while based somewhat on the Wright and Snell (1998) conceptualization of HR flexibility, used scales that diverged from that conceptualization. Bhattacharya et al. (2005) assessed the HR practice, skill, and behaviour flexibility, but did not distinguish between resource and coordination flexibility, and a number of later studies used that scale or a variation of it. In what is the most thorough scale validation to date, Way et al. (2015) developed an HR flexibility scale tied directly to, and expanding on, the resource and coordination flexibility of HR practices, skills, and behaviours. Using seven separate samples, these authors demonstrated the content validity, internal consistency reliability, convergent validity, discriminant validity, and criterion-related validity of their measure. In the end, their measure consisted of 21 items and five factors: Resource Flexibility in HR Practices (five items), Resource Flexibility in Employee Skills and Behaviours (four items), Coordination Flexibility in HR Practices (four items), Coordination Flexibility in Contingent Worker Skills and Behaviours (four items), and Coordination Flexibility in Employee Skills and Behaviours (four items). It is important to note that, contrary to the original Wright and Snell (1998) model, the employee skills and behaviours were not separate, but converged with one another, and also that this measure went beyond their model to include contingent workers.

More recently, Way et al. (2018) pointed out an inconsistency in much of the work on HR flexibility. They noted that the basic theory underlying the importance of flexibility suggests that it is most critical in highly volatile environments. This (returning to our previous discussion of fit as moderation) suggests that the dynamicity of the environment moderates the relationship between HR flexibility and performance, such that the relationship is positive in dynamic environments, but perhaps even negative in stable ones. In essence, they argue that *flexibility may be a firm asset in some cases, but a liability in others*. However, all of the previous research examining the direct relationship between HR flexibility and performance always treated it as an asset. The results from Way et al. (2018) show first that a flexible business strategy and HPWS serve as precursors to HR flexibility, and second that industry dynamism and growth moderate the relationship between HR flexibility and financial performance.

Another variable to consider is 'interaction orientation'. Ma et al. (2019) examined this as a potential driver of organization performance through HR flexibility. They defined interaction orientation as ' … a firm's capability to interact with its individual customers and to utilize the knowledge obtained through those successive interactions towards the achievement of profitable customer relationships' (p. 333). In a study of 156 companies in China, they found that interaction orientation was positively related to performance through HR flexibility.

The potential mediating role of 'HR flexibility' in the relationship between HPWS and organizational performance was examined by Katou et al. (2021). Using Beltran-Martin et al.'s (2008) conceptualization of HR flexibility as consisting of functional flexibility, skill malleability, and behavioural flexibility, they used a longitudinal Greek database to explore this relationship. They found that HPWS positively impacts all three components of HR flexibility. However, the strongest effect on organization performance was through skills malleability, with a smaller effect through behavioural flexibility, and almost no effect through functional flexibility.

Finally, Way et al. (2023) examined both the mediating role of HR flexibility in the HPWS-performance relationship and the moderating role of organization size in the relationship between HR flexibility and performance. Using a global sample of 8,139 individuals across 306 companies, they first found support for the mediating role of HR flexibility in the relationship between HPWS and performance, somewhat replicating the results of Beltran-Martin et al. (2008) and Katou et al. (2021). More interestingly, they found that the positive relationship between HR flexibility and performance was strongest for large companies and weakest for small companies. When separating out the different components of the overall performance measure (employee, organization, customer, and financial outcomes), they actually found that HR flexibility was negatively related to financial performance for small companies.

The literature on HR flexibility continues to grow and develop. From the earliest theoretical conceptualizations of HR flexibility, through a number of empirical examinations of its direct relationship with firm performance, to the newer, more theoretically accurate research suggesting dynamism as a moderator of the relationship between HR flexibility and performance, research has become much more rigorous and theoretically accurate.

Most studies have found a positive relationship between HR flexibility (however conceptualized) and performance. But some recent research has cautioned that flexibility is not always a clear asset. Recent findings provide additional avenues for future research. Given the fact that most believe that the VUCA characteristics in markets will continue to grow, rather than shrink, HR flexibility will become even more important to organizations, and research in this area will continue to be important.

Conclusions

In Chapter 2 of this book, we discussed the extensive literature on the relationship between HR practices and performance outcomes. This relationship has been well documented and it has been extended by exploring mediating mechanisms such as organizational commitment. In this present chapter, focusing on fit and flexibility, we have explored the relationship in even greater depth. First, we note that SHRM encompasses a firm's strategy, its HR practices, and the skills and behaviours of employees. However, for SHRM to live up to its name, it must tie strategy to HR practices and workforce characteristics, which led us to the concept of 'fit'. We showed that according to the most popular view of fit, i.e., fit as moderation, there is little support for the fact that fit matters to performance. However, we also noted that this is likely due more to the generic level at which most HR practices are measured. Thus, future research that more specifically captures the products or outcomes necessary for a strategy is much needed in order for our empirical work to support what most firms do in practice.

Then we turned our attention to HR flexibility, which is viewed as a firm-level construct encompassing the resource and coordination flexibility of a firm's HR practices, employee skills, and employee behaviours. Flexibility is conceptualized as *the ability of a firm to achieve fit with a diverse and changing set of circumstances*. The research on fit has generally used the HR practices, employee skills, and employee behaviours model, but the operationalization has not been consistent. However, regardless of operationalization, measures of flexibility have consistently demonstrated positive relationships with performance, even though the theory would suggest that the positive relationship should only be observed in environments characterized as VUCA. The study by Way et al. (2023) noted how flexibility can be an asset in some contexts but a liability in other contexts. This, and other recent studies of fit and flexibility in SHRM, suggests that there is scope for further productive research in this area.

7   A stock-take and promising avenues for future research

The previous six chapters have tracked research in the field of Strategic Human Resource Management over a period of half a century. As a result, two main questions arise: first, what overall conclusions can be drawn from this body of research, and second, what are the emergent issues meriting future research?

One of the notable developments has been the unravelling, in many corporations, but not all, of the sophisticated packages of SHRM which had been celebrated and portrayed in the 1980s. In the face of more severe global competition and the squeeze on costs, some firms, including such notable and celebrated cases as Hewlett Packard, proceeded to erode many of the attributes of the high-commitment model of HRM (Hodgson et al. 2012). As the prevalence of 'low road' practices developed, the headlines were increasingly characterized by reports of precarious work and poor working conditions. We noted the increased polarized distribution of workers in high-paid and low-paid jobs as indicative of this trend. While low wages characterize many parts of modern economies, there are pockets of very high compensation such as at Facebook and Google where the median compensation in 2022 was nearly $300,000 (*Wall Street Journal* 2022). Fragmentation and turbulence – reflected in the volatility, uncertainty, complexity, and ambiguity phenomenon – seem to characterize the state of play in modern employment conditions. But there is a possibility this generalization rests on an unrepresentative set of highly publicized cases.

From another point of view, it could be said that the basic underlying issues in SHRM remain broadly familiar, even though not presenting in quite the same way. As noted in the introductory chapter, some core themes of HRM are perennial and have been revisited and reworked several times under different guises. Examples include the Resource-Based View, High-Performance Working, Talent Management, and the new focus on 'Management Practices' (Bloom and Van Reenen 2007; Bender et al. 2018). At the core is the *employment relationship*. Employers seek

DOI: 10.4324/9781003364276-8

reliable service; employees seek fair rewards. From an employer's perspective, a workforce must be found, recruited, selected, trained, objectives set, performance monitored, compensation provided, and in due course, contracts terminated. From these basics, many variants emerge. The employer may sub-contract and so the identity of the 'actual' employer may be uncertain and a matter for legal determination. Likewise, whether an employment contract even exists or whether there is some form of payment for service from a supposedly 'self-employed' contractor, also becomes a matter of contention. Relatedly, the fluctuation from a commitment to a control-based relationship and back again is a further instance of continuity. However, when taking a long view, the recent increased prevalence of precarious forms of low-paid work sitting alongside a privileged few attracting high rewards can be seen as far from new. Moreover, while the precise list of items in the HR bundles may vary, the fundamental conceptualization of what constitutes the domain of SHRM has remained broadly the same. The early models and their building blocks of vertical and horizontal integration, the positioning of workers as 'assets' rather than mere 'costs', and the strategic value of the intelligent use of human resources as the basis of value-added are all concepts which have endured. There remains scope for debate about whether the field has narrowed unhealthily (Kaufman 2015) or whether it has matured and deepened (Wright et al. 2015), but the enduring significance of the core concepts seems evident.

But, as noted earlier, an alternative conceptualization of the focal issue of concern seeks to shift attention from a single firm perspective with its own approach to managing its employment relations to a perspective which expands the unit of analysis to encompass a wider 'eco-systems' of interdependent agents. New technologies and project work forms tend to favour cross-boundary working (Snell et al. 2023; Roundy and Burke-Smalley 2022). This kind of network analysis is however not entirely new as many of its insights were presaged in earlier publications – for example, research on network organizations (Miles and Snow 1986; Snow 1992; Storey 1998). Nonetheless, it does seem likely that contemporary conditions of turbulence and new digital technologies such as online labour platforms (OLPs) will impel and enable new forms of work organization which extend beyond conventional organizational boundaries (Keegan and Meijerink 2023) which favour complex adaptive systems (Burke and Morley 2023).

As noted in the first chapter, the very idea of 'strategy' in HRM implies considerable scope for, and the exercise of, *choice*. HR specialists, or indeed other managers making decisions which impact on employment, have the potential to make choices about the kinds of employment – and employment relations – they want to encourage and realize (though this does not mean their choices are unfettered). As noted in previous chapters, there are the classic strategic choices about a high value-added/high-pay model or a low-cost/low-pay business model. 'Alignment' in strategic HR is used to imply matching high-quality customer service with high-end employment practices built on skilled staff, good training, and high commitment. To some extent that equation may still hold. But, as noted in Chapter 5, in recent times there is evidence that even high-end employers have fragmented their labour forces so that some staff are retained on low-end conditions such as zero-hour contracts, low pay, and poor terms and conditions, while others are highly rewarded (Weil 2014). The extent to which HR strategists (or those managers acting in that capacity) have the scope and freedom of manoeuvre to resist the pressures created by low-cost options (such as outsourcing to low-cost economies, or contracting out certain service functions) is often unclear. This topic would make for an excellent future research project. The boundary conditions to open choice are increasingly fuzzy. This means that the work HR specialists are expected to do fluctuates over time even while, at a more fundamental level, it broadly remains the same. The data on changing HR competencies as reported in Chapter 4 suggests that persons occupying these roles are expected to play an increasingly strategic role in place of an administrative one. But the extent to which the choices they make are context-dependent remains uncertain and more empirical research is required.

While the fundamentals of SHRM remain in place as a reference point for practice and theory, it is evident, as noted throughout the book, that there are many counterforces which are in contention with the rather more optimistic outlook of the early days of the field. Instead of an overall drift towards the adoption of many of the attributes of SHRM which was recorded empirically through extensive fieldwork in mainstream companies and documented in detail (Storey 1992), in many instances, the tidal flow since then has often been in the reverse direction. Financialization, fragmented labour markets, deteriorations in terms and conditions of work, outsourcing, and short-termism have been compelling forces which fly in the face of the high-commitment model of SHRM. Signs of employers taking the 'low road' option have been all too evident (Osterman 2018). And yet examples of employers taking the 'high road' still do exist and there is evidence that they can 'do well by doing good' (Osterman 2018).

Are there signs of progression in HR theorizing?

A review of HR theorizing such as has been attempted in this short book raises the question as to whether there has been any significant progression in theory (as opposed to further empirical affirmations of existing theory)? This is a contested terrain. There are certainly indications of changing concerns and shifting foci. HRM and TQM, The War for

Talent, Employee Engagement, and many other themes have entered centre stage for short periods before giving way to 'new' focal concerns. But whether a case can be made for cumulative progression is a more open question. A gloomy assessment is made by Kaufman (2020). His bleak judgement is one of limited progress beyond the initial contributions and a series of either trivial or replicating studies in the subsequent years. He refutes the claims of HR journal editors and suggests that:

'Strategic HRM's 30-year knowledge outputs, at least with a high-oomph factor (and not a rediscovery/repackaging of earlier-known ideas, such as strategic HRM, high-commitment model, and participative management; Kaufman 2008, 2012), effectively drops to zero' (p. 65).

As a result, Kaufman (2020) contends that there is, overall, a 'contribution deficit':

We still have, particularly in the U.S. case, almost no idea of how many firms have implemented a partial or full HPWS (5%, 40%, or 70%?), whether the trend is increasing, decreasing or flat, the HPWS success/ failure rate, what other types/configurations of HRM systems populate the economy, and whether the HPWS (now 40 years old) is still a relevant model or has evolved into something distinctly different. [There is] … a dearth of case studies and field research—approaching near-zero in U.S. management and HR journals—of the system's structure, practices, and operation in real-world companies … or meaningful consideration of business/organisational trends, such as widespread erosion of internal labour markets, financialisation's bias against longer term HPWS-type investments, effect of business cycles/ crises and growth rates … . (2020, p. 65).

This is a harsh evaluation. The reference to the relative lack of meaningful research projects in the USA is neglectful of the number of studies in that country and of the wider body of international research especially as conducted in Europe and Asia.

But there are other critical views, some of which attack from a different angle. For example, Butterick et al. (2021) contend that 'some aspects of HRM theory (Atkinson 1984; Lepak and Snell 1999) have acted as transmission mechanisms for wider political and economic forces driving persistent economic inequalities and legitimising the increasing commodification of labour' (p. 848). This suggests that HRM theorizing itself may inadvertently reinforce negative trends. Indeed, these critics go further, they argue that 'Pervasive ideological individualism (Dundon and Rafferty 2018) has contributed to widespread amorality (Quade et al. 2020) in people management' (Butterick and Charlwood 2021, p. 848).

As even these few examples of recent overall assessments of HR research suggest, there are some serious and deep-seated issues to be considered as research in HRM progresses to the next stage.

What next?

So, to address our second question: what next? What issues and themes will future researchers in SHRM be studying? We cannot of course predict the future, but we can report on current and emergent themes in the very latest literature and other influential sources such as conference agendas, consultancy reports, workshops, and grey literature such as think-tank reports and government-sponsored reports. These sources offer different windows through which to view the nature of contemporary trends and concerns. The view from these windows varies: some disclose a bright optimistic landscape others a darker more pessimistic view.

In what follows, we first draw out the key issues found in emergent academic literature; second, we summarize findings from the grey literature of think-tank and government reports; third, we review themes found in practitioner-oriented publications such as *Harvard Business Review* and *HR Magazine*; and finally, we seek to encapsulate the key contemporary and future-oriented issues as found represented in contemporary practitioner settings and forums.

These diverse sources of insight do not always produce agreement on what is happening in SHRM and what are the central research issues. But from this plurality, a number of interesting and important research agendas can be constructed.

For the first of these, the review of the very latest academic literature, we consulted the following journals: *Asia Pacific Journal of Human Resource Management, Human Resource Management Journal, Human Resource Management, Human Relations, International Journal of Human Relations, Academy of Management Journal*, and the *Journal of Chinese Human Resource Management*. We included 'online-first' articles i.e., those issued prior to full publication.

Of interest to note are the topics that had dropped off the radar or which had received lesser attention than previously. Compared with past times, there has been much less discussion about the nature and role of human resource management as a function and its relationship with personnel management; likewise, the erstwhile foci on the relation between HRM and Total Quality Management, Learning Organizations and Corporate Culture have given way to other concerns.

Notable themes of *continuity* included high-performance work systems (HPWS), leadership, citizenship behaviour, women and careers, diversity and inclusion, organizational change, organizational climate, commitment, work and identity, labour-management partnerships, employee engagement and the psychological contract, HR practices in knowledge-intensive firms, freelance, and temporary and agency work.

With hindsight, it can be observed that there have been some false dawns. For example, around 2014–2016 there was considerable speculation about the significance of neuroscience for human resource management. A CIPD report suggested it was an 'emerging but rapidly growing field' (2014b, p. 3). The evidence base for this was anecdotal, and the practitioners extolling the approach were attracted to the 'scientific' credentials that it seemed to convey. From the perspective of 2023, it is notable that research into the neuroscience applications to human resource management over the intervening years has been scarce. The potential remains of course for future research advances in this domain.

Emerging with new, or renewed, emphasis is workforce analytics (Angrave et al. 2016; Huselid 2018); the use of artificial intelligence in HR (Palos-Sánchez et al. (2022); attention to human resource management in times of disruption and crises; disability (Bacon and Hoque 2022) and other aspects of equality, diversity and inclusion (EDI) (Noon and Ogbonna 2021); signalling theory (Garavan et al. 2022; Guest et al. 2021); and deeper dives into the *processes* of HR practice. Corruption, risk, terrorism, and management in contexts of high uncertainty, volatility, violence, economic crises, and natural disasters all now find a presence. Signalling theory, a key theme in economics, has only recently made an appearance in HRM – for example, Garavan et al. (2022), Guest et al. (2021), Connelly et al. (2011), Chang and Hyun Chin (2018), Pudil et al. (2018) and Pernkopf et al. (2021). In the context of HRM, signalling theory has clear relevance to recruitment. Recruitment messages from employers and signals from employees such as qualifications and selected experiences are cases in point. More broadly, signalling theory places focus on 'line managers as signallers of HR messages and employees as receivers' (Guest et al. 2021: 796). The gap between policy and practice (the black box) can be approached from this theoretical perspective. Thus, the 'strength' of the signals can be assessed alongside variables such as coherence of the messages received.

Features such as the distinctiveness of the signal, visibility, clarity, frequency, consistency, understandability, and relevance of HR practices to goal achievement are brought into focus alongside aspects of employee perceptions.

For example, Pernkopf et al. (2021) use signalling theory to interpret the recruiting process. They note how traditional recruiting activities are marked by information asymmetry and uncertainty among applicants. The researchers note how new technologies change the picture and how applicants interpret the signals available. Their results show 'that while congruent signals increase employer attractiveness and mixed-signal situations reduce it, distinct evaluative patterns emerge when potential applicants reflect and judge employers' (2021: 392).

Further research on signal strength and HR attributions is reported by Meier-Barthold et al. (2022). Employees' perceptions about the intentions behind their organization's HR practices are shown to be important. The 'content' of an HR system and the processes of communicating this content drive employees' attributions. This article forms part of a wider body of recent work related to explicating the mechanisms and processes involved in linking HR policies and practices to signalling theory and employee perceptions and attributions (e.g., Guest et al. 2021; Alfes et al. 2021). Future research opportunities arise in relation to contexts where HR signals may be weak, ambiguous, or even contradictory. Likewise, research in Australian emergency service organizations illustrates how reliability-seeking organizations such as these require alignment between HR policies and the challenges and priorities they face (Kellner et al. 2023).

There is extensive speculation about the potential impact of automation and artificial intelligence as these technologies spread across industrial sectors and occupational categories, but these concerns have seemingly not yet been fully evidenced in the mainstream HR journals. From these journals, it is difficult to see any new themes which are assuming a position of dominance. That said, a much wider range of current issues is to be found in journals such as *Industrial & Labor Relations Review* and *Organization Studies*, each of which tackles wider economic and social trends beyond human resource management practice directly. Likewise, big-picture issues, as reported in earlier chapters, are found reflected in a number of research monographs. For example, the review of precarious work in six advanced economies by Arne Kalleberg highlighted the significant fact that while precarious work was characteristic of virtually all societies historically, the recent growth of this form of employment after decades of social progress represents a momentous reversal of trends in the management of work (Kalleberg 2018). Few studies nowadays report the kind of diffusion of SHRM policies and practices of the kind found some decades ago. As Kalleberg notes, it is all too easy to paint a dystopian future for work; the key lesson is to seek ways to shape positive work design of the kind described by Osterman with regard to care workers (Osterman 2017). This is a key agenda item for human resource managers of the future.

Our second source, the think-tank and government-sponsored reports, presents yet another, and rather different, perspective on contemporary HR-related topics. An important example from the UK is the report *Good Work: The Taylor Review of Modern Working Practices*

(Taylor 2018). This is the report of the independent review of employment practices in the modern economy commissioned by the Prime Minister. We referred to this publication in Chapter 5. The report notes the historically high levels of participation in the labour market and observes that the UK has one of the most flexible labour markets in the world. It records a notable shift towards more flexible forms of working, yet full-time, permanent work still constitutes most of the employment in the UK (63.0%). The review finds that flexible work benefits some people and that it helps maintain high levels of employment. But it does not work for everyone, and the report records many problems stemming from poor employment practices associated with precarious work and the gig economy (Taylor 2018, p. 27).

Public policy and labour law have been behind the curve in relation to these developments in most countries. In Canada, the Ministry of Labour for Ontario commissioned a *Changing Workplaces Review* to respond to the secular shift towards precarious work. This initiative stemmed from a concern that existing labour laws were not adequate for dealing with the new fragmented and precarious employment landscape (Mitchell and Murray 2017). The report offered tentative suggestions and indicated the need to approach new forms of regulation with some caution.

The sources found by looking through the third window into contemporary and future-oriented themes, i.e., the practitioner-oriented magazines (such as *Harvard Business Review* and *HR Magazine*) tend to put the spotlight on practical and positive activity. For example, *HR Magazine* in its 2022–2023 editions covered topics such as creating loyalty among employees, positive action regarding LGBT+; HR's role in promoting more representative socio-economic representation; and policy developments activity in relation to the menopause. The *Harvard Business Review* has, in the past, published some significant articles that have shaped the HR debate – notably, for example, the landmark article 'From Control to Commitment' (Walton 1985). But recent issues of this journal have devoted less space to mainstream HR topics of a policy nature and shifted instead to more tactical people-management concerns.

Fourth and finally, a different perspective on the present and the future can be gleaned by drawing on a different well-spring: that is, interpretations from the practitioner interface. From our various engagements with senior managers in a wide range of industry sectors and country settings, we are able to construct a picture of the kind of issues which occupy the concerns of contemporary practitioners.

As noted in earlier chapters of this book, context matters a great deal. Accordingly, emergent themes and issues are likely to be situationally related. Patrick Wright, as part of his direct engagement with senior practitioners, has observed that in several leading corporations in the USA, a notable development is the changing expectations placed on the leaders of the HR function. In the USA, these leaders are increasingly termed the Chief HR Officer (CHRO). Whereas previously CHROs only sometimes directly reported to the Chief Executive Officer (CEO), and only rarely dealt with the wider board of directors, today they tend almost always to report directly to the CEO and they also frequently interact with other directors on the board. This trend has been driven by three factors. First, the 'War for Talent' placed human capital on the radar screen of CEOs, and they have consequently demanded that the CHRO oversee the delivery of talent to the firm. Second, numerous corporate scandals focused the attention of directors on the remuneration packages of their CEO and how these might drive dysfunctional decision-making. Thus, boards increasingly rely on the CHRO as the interface between them and the CEO in the process of setting pay. Third, some high-profile failures of CEOs have caused board members to recognize CEO succession as one of their most important governance responsibilities. Increasingly, CHROs act as the liaison among the board members, the incumbent CEO, and the potential CEO candidates. All these factors have increased both the visibility and importance of the CHRO. Research agendas for the future in this regard thus relate to the variety of ways in which CHROs are playing this more critical role, what competencies are required, and what difference they are making.

Paradoxically, a significant current theme in many contexts is how occupants of senior HR positions are perceiving and responding to the many cost-saving pressures catalogued in this book. Despite the many reversals from high-road practices and towards low-road practices that have been noted, there has been a surprising paucity of investigations tracking the part played by the HR function in these processes. High-profile spokespersons for the profession tend not to talk openly about the pressures they and their colleagues face; and academic researchers have, in the main, not yet got around to shedding light on these matters.

Future-oriented research agendas

So, taking all of the above sources into account, the future research agenda(s) for the domain of strategic human resource management remains open and wide ranging. Many of the big, long-standing issues remain unresolved and ripe for imaginative forms of investigation. Which forms and combinations of fit and flexibility are conducive to performance outcomes? Which forms of workforce management can yield sustained profitability? Can the forms which are economically viable also (to adapt Osterman's phrase) 'do good while doing well'? How much scope for choice about HR strategy really exists under contemporaneous conditions when competition is heightened because of global reach through technology and a highly mobile international labour supply? Can the high-end practices extend into industry sectors which have become conventionally subject to low-wage casualised labour such as catering, retail, hotels, and elderly care? Do the opportunities for mutual gains extend far enough to allow the inherent costs of the high-commitment model to be offset by the positive outcomes such as loyalty, commitment, lower absence, and the like? What role will be played in the future by collective forms of worker representation alongside the more individualized forms?

Likewise, what is the future role for state regulation? Running in parallel with each of these questions is a second-order set of questions concerning how HR specialists act in relation to them. Do they seek to set the agenda, or more passively react to imperatives established by more powerful members of executive teams? Framing this question in another way: how are employment policies constructed and how will they be in the future? What kinds of values and logics are built into the process? Implicit in these kinds of questions, but in some ways extending to a level beyond, are research agendas which tackle higher-level political and economic issues concerning, for example, the influence wielded by investors in their various forms – venture capitalists, managerial buyouts, stock markets, pension funds, hedge funds, private investors, banks, and peer-to-peer lenders. Nested within these 'big questions' remain a host of traditional research areas and these are likely to remain relevant: recruitment and selection practices, training and development provision, diverse forms of compensation, forms of workforce engagement, and similar enduring issues. Whatever the future may hold, there is clearly no shortage of rich research themes for scholars of SHRM to pursue.

References

Abbot, A. (1988). *The System of Professions: An Essay on the Division of Expert Labor*. Chicago, IL: University of Chicago Press.

Abernathy, W. J. (1978). *The Productivity Dilemma*. Baltimore, MD: Johns Hopkins University Press.

Abowd, J. M., Kramarz, F. & Margolis, D. (1999). 'High wage workers and high wage firms'. *Econometrica, 67*(2): 251–333.

Adams L. (2016). 'Kissing goodbye to Ulrich: Next generation HR organisation design'. *Disruptive HR*. Available at: http://disruptivehr.co.uk/2016/05/10/kissing-goodbye-to-ulrich/ (Accessed: January 2, 2019).

Aguinis, H. & O'Boyle, E. (2014). 'Star performers in twenty-first century organizations'. *Personnel Psychology, 67*: 313–350.

Alfes, K., Veld, M. & Fürstenberg, N. (2021) 'The relationship between perceived high- performance work systems, combinations of human resource well-being, and human resource performance attributions and engagement'. *Human Resource Management Journal, 31*(3):729–752.

Ali, M. *et al.* (2022). 'Green intellectual capital, green HRM and green social identity toward sustainable environment: A new integrated framework for Islamic banks', *International Journal of Manpower, 43*(3): 614–638. Available at: 10.1108/IJM-04-2020-0185

Alvaredo, F., Chancel, L., Piketty, T., Saez, E. & Zucman, G. (2018). *World Inequality Report 2018*. Boston, MA: Harvard Business School Press.

Alzgool, M., R. H. (2019). 'Nexus between green HRM and green management towards fostering green values'. *Management Science Letters, 9*(12): 2073–2082.

Anderson, B., Poeschel, F. & Ruhs, M. (2021). 'Rethinking labour migration: Covid-19, essential work, and systemic resilience'. *Comparative Migration Studies, 9*(45): 1–19

Andriopoulos, C. & Lewis, M. W. (2009). 'Exploitation-exploration tensions and organizational ambidexterity: Managing paradoxes of innovation'. *Organization Science, 20*: 696–717.

Angrave, D., Charlwood, A., Kirkpatrick, I., Lawrence, M. & Stuart, M. (2016). 'HR and analytics: Why HR is set to fail the big data challenge'. *Human Resource Management Journal, 26*(1): 1–11.

Appelbaum, E. & Batt, R. (2014). *Private Equity at Work: When Wall Street Manages Main Street*. New York: Russell Sage Foundation.

Appelbaum, E., Bailey, T., Berg, P. & Kalleberg, A. (2000). *Manufacturing Advantage: Why High-Performance Work Systems Pay Off.* Ithaca, NY: ILR Press.

Argote, L. & Miron-Spektor, E. (2011). 'Organizational learning: From experience to knowledge'. *Organization Science, 22*(5): 1123–1137.

Argyris, C. & Schon, D. (1981). *Organizational Learning.* Reading, MA: Addison-Wesley.

Arnold, J. (1997). *Managing Careers in the 21st Century.* London: Paul Chapman.

Arthur, J. B. (1992). 'The link between business strategy and industrial relations systems in American steel minimills'. *Industrial and Labor Relations Review, 45*: 488–506

Arthur, J. B. (1994). 'Effects of human resource systems on manufacturing performance and turnover'. *Academy of Management Journal, 37*(3): 670–687.

Arthur, M. B. & Rousseau, D. M. (1996). *The Boundaryless Career: A New Employment Principle for a New Organizational Era.* Oxford: Oxford University Press.

Atkins, A. (2018). *Inequality: What Can Be Done?* Boston: Harvard University Press.

Atkinson, J. (1984). 'Manpower strategies for flexible organisations'. *Personnel Management, 16*: 28–31.

Autor, D., Dorn, D., Katz, L. F., Patterson, C. & Van Reenen, J. (2017). *The Fall of the Labor Share and the Rise of Superstar Firms.* Boston, MA: MIT.

Bacon, N. & Hoque, K. (2022). 'The treatment of disabled individuals in small, medium-sized, and large firms'. *Human Resource Management, 61*(2), 137–156

Baird, L. & Meshoulam, I. (1988). 'Managing two fits of strategic human resource management'. *Academy of Management Review, 13*(1): 116–128.

Barney, J. (1991). 'Firm resources and sustained competitive advantage'. *Journal of Management, 17*(1): 99–120.

Barney, J. & Wright, P. (1998). 'On becoming a strategic partner: Examining the role of human resources in gaining competitive advantage'. *Human Resource Management Journal, 37*(1): 31–46.

Batt, R. (2002). 'Managing customer services: Human resource practices, quit rates, and sales growth'. *Academy of Management Journal, 45*(3): 587–597.

Batt, R. & Appelbaum, E. (2013). *The Impact of Financialization on Management and Employment Outcomes.* Kalamazoo, MI: Upjohn Institute.

Batt, R., Holman, D. & Holtgrew, U. (2009). 'The globalization of service work: Comparative institutional perspectives on call centres'. *Industrial and Labor Relations Review, 62*(4): 453–488.

Becker, B. & Gerhart, B. (1996). 'The impact of human resource management on organizational performance: Progress and prospects'. *Academy of Management Journal, 39*(4): 779–801.

Becker, B. & Huselid, M. (1998). 'High performance work systems and firm performance: A synthesis of research and managerial implications'. *Research in Personnel and Human Resources, 16*(1): 53–101.

Becker, B. E. & Huselid, M. A. (2006). 'Strategic human resources management: Where do we go from here?' *Journal of Management, 32*(6): 898–925.

Becker, G. (1964). *Human Capital Theory.* Chicago, IL: University of Chicago Press.

Beckhard, R. & Harris, R. T. (1987). *Organizational Transitions: Managing Complex Change* (2nd edition). Reading, MA: Addison-Wesley.

Beechler, S. & Woodward, I. (2009). 'The global war for talent'. *Journal of International Management, 15*: 273–285.

Beer, M., Spector, B., Lawrence, P., Mills, D. & Walton, R. (1985). *Human Resources Management: A General Managers Perspective*. New York: Free Press.

Beijer S., Peccei R., van Veldhoven M. & Paauwe J. (2019). 'The turn to employees in the measurement of human resource practices: A critical review and proposed way forward'. *Human Resource Management Journal, 31*(1): 1–17.

Beletskiy and Fey (2021). 'HR ambidexterity and absorptive capacities: A paradox-based approach to HRM capabilities and practice adoption in MNC subsidiaries'. *Human Resource Management, 60*: 863–883.

Beltrán-Martín, I., Bou-Llusar, J. C. & Salvador-Gómez, A. (2021). 'HR flexibility and firm performance in professional service firms'. *Journal of Management & Organization, First view online*: pages 1–22. 10.1017/jmo.2021.5

Beltrán-Martín, I., Roca-Puig, V., Escrig-Tena, A. & Bou-Llusar, J. C. (2008). 'Human resource flexibility as a mediating variable between high performance work systems and performance'. *Journal of Management, 34*(5): 1009–1044.

Bender, S., Bloom, N., Card, D., Van Reenen, J. & Wolter, S. (2018). 'Management practices, workforce selection and productivity'. *Journal of Labor Economics, 36*(S1): 371–409.

Benner, M. J. & Tushman, M. L. (2003). 'Exploitation, exploration and process management: The productivity dilemma revisited'. *Academy of Management Review, 28*: 238–256.

Bersin, J. (2016). 'The HR software market reinvents itself'. *Forbes*. July 18. https://www.forbes.com/sites/joshbersin/2016/07/18/the-hr-software-market-reinvents-itself/.

Bessa, I. & Tomlinson, J. (2017). 'Established, accelerated and emergent themes in flexible work research'. *Journal of Industrial Relations, 59*(2): 153–169.

Bhattacharya, M., Gibson, D. E. & Doty, D. H. (2005). 'The effects of flexibility in employee skills, employee behaviors, and human resource practices on firm performance'. *Journal of Management, 31*(4): 622–640.

Birkinshaw, J. & Gibson, C. (2004). 'Building ambidexterity into an organization'. *MIT Sloan Management Review*, Summer: 47–55.

Blau, G. J. (1986). 'Job involvement and organizational commitment as interactive predictors of tardiness and absenteeism'. *Journal of Management, 12*: 577–584.

Blau, P. (1964). *Exchange and Power in Social Life*. New York: Wiley.

Bloodworth, J. (2018). *Hired: Six Months Undercover in Low Wage Britain*. London: Atlantic Books.

Bloom, N. & Van Reenen, J. (2007). 'Measuring and explaining management practices across firms and countries'. *The Quarterly Journal of Economics, 122*(4): 1351–1408.

Bloom, N., Sadun, R. & Van Reenen, J. (2012). 'Does management really work?' *Harvard Business Review*, November: 77–82.

Boudreau, J. & Ramstad, P. (2005). 'Talentship, talent segmentation and sustainability: A new HR decision science paradigm for a new strategy definition'. *Human Resource Management, 44*(2): 129–136.

Boudreau, J. W. & Ramstad, P. M. (2009). 'Beyond HR: Extending the paradigm through a talent decision science'. In Storey, J., Wright, P. M. & Ulrich, D. (eds),

The Routledge Companion to Strategic Human Resource Management. Abingdon, UK, and New York: Routledge.

Bowen, D. E. & Ostroff, C. (2004). 'Understanding HRM-firm performance linkages: The role of the "strength" of the HRM system'. *Academy of Management Review, 29*(2): 203–221.

Boxall, P., Purcell, J. & Wright, P. M. (2008). 'Human resource management: Scope, analysis, and significance'. In Boxall, P., Purcell, J. & Wright, P. M. (eds), *The Oxford Handbook of Human Resource Management.* Oxford: Oxford University Press.

Boyatzis, R. (1982). *The Competent Manager: A Model for Effective Performance.* New York: Wiley.

Bracken, D., Church, A., Fleenor, J. & Rose, D. (eds) (2018). *The Handbook of Strategic 360 Feedback.* Oxford: Oxford University Press.

Brennecke, J. & Stoemmer, N. (2018). 'The network-performance relationship in knowledge-intensive contexts: Meta-analysis and cross-level comparison'. *Human Resource Management, 57*(1): 11–36.

Brown, S. & Eisenhardt, K. (1998). *Competing on the Edge: Strategy as Structured Chaos.* Boston, MA: Harvard Business School Press.

Bryar, C. & Carr, B. (2022). *Working Backwards: Insights, Stories and Secrets from Inside Amazon.* London: Macmillan.

Budhwar, P., Cumming & Wood, G. (2022). 'Entrepreneurial finance and the legacy of Mike Wright'. *British Journal of Management, 33*(1): 3–8

Burke, C. M. & Morley, M. J. (2023). 'Toward a non-organizational theory of human resource management? A complex adaptive systems perspective on the human resource management ecosystem in (con) temporary organizing'. *Human Resource Management, 62*(1): 31–53.

Butterick, M. & Charlwood, A. (2021). 'HRM and the COVID-19 pandemic: How can we stop making a bad situation worse?' *Human Resource Management Journal, 31*(4): 847–856.

Calder, S. (2022). 'P&O Ferries defends brutal sacking of 800 staff'. *Independent,* 13th March.

Caldwell, R. (2003). 'The changing roles of personnel managers: Old ambiguities, new uncertainties'. *Journal of Management Studies, 40*(4): 983–1004.

Cappelli, P. & Keller, J. (2013). 'Classifying work in the new economy'. *Academy of Management Review, 38*(4): 575–596.

Cappelli, P. & Neumark, D. (2001). 'Do "high-performance" work practices improve establishment-level outcomes?' *Industrial & Labor Relations Review, 54*(4): 737–775.

Cascio, W. & Boudreau, J. (2011). *Investing in People: The Financial Impact of Human Resource Initiatives.* Upper Saddle, NJ: Pearson.

Chadwick, C. & Li, P. (2018). 'HR systems, HR departments, and perceived establishment labor productivity'. *Human Resource Management, 57*(6): 1415–1428. doi: 10.1002/hrm.21914.

Chadwick, C., Way, S. A., Kerr, G. & Thacker, J. W. (2013). 'Boundary conditions of the high-investment human resource systems: Small-firm labor productivity relationship'. *Personnel Psychology, 66*: 311–343.

Chambers, E. G., Foulon, M., Handfield-Jones, H., Hankin, S. M. & Michaels, E. G. (1998). 'The war for talent'. *McKinsey Quarterly, 3*: 44–57.

Chandler, A. (1962). *Strategy and Structure*. Boston, MA: MIT Press.

Chang E. & Hyun Chin, H. (2018). 'Signaling or experiencing: Commitment HRM effects on recruitment and employees' online ratings'. *Journal of Business Research, 84*: 18–175.

Chang, S., Gong, Y., Way, S. A. & Jia, L. (2013). 'Flexibility-oriented HRM systems, absorptive capacity, and market responsiveness and firm innovativeness'. *Journal of Management, 39*(7): 1924–1951.

Choonara, J., Margia, A. & Carmo, R. M. (eds). (2022). *Faces of Precarity: Critical Perspectives on Work, Subjectivities and Struggles*. Bristol: Bristol University Press.

Chuang, C. H., Jackson, S. E. & Jiang, Y. (2016). 'Can knowledge-intensive teamwork be managed? Examining the roles of HRM systems, leadership, and tacit knowledge'. *Journal of Management. 42*(2): 524–554.

Chuang, C. H. & Liao, H. (2010). 'Strategic human resource management in service context: Taking care of business by taking care of employees and customers'. *Personnel Psychology, 63*(1): 153–196.

Chung, G. H. & Pak, J. (2021). 'Is there internal fit among ability-, motivation-, and opportunity-enhancing HR practices? Evidence from South Korea'. *Review of Managerial Science, 15*: 2049–2074. 10.1007/s11846-020-00415-y

CIPD (2022). 'The CIPD Professional Map'. Available at: https://peopleprofession.cipd.org/profession-map#gref / (Accessed: Feb 1st 2023).

CIPD (2022). 'Business Partnering'. Available at: https://www.cipd.co.uk/knowledge/fundamentals/people/hr/business-partnering-factsheet (Accessed: Feb 1st 2023).

CIPD (2014). *Neuroscience in Action: Applying Insight to L&D Practice*. Research Report, London: CIPD.

CIPD (2022). *Talent Management*. Factsheet. Available at: https://www.cipd.co.uk/knowledge/strategy/resourcing/talent-factsheet#gref (Accessed November 29, 2022)

CIPD Factsheet (2017). 'Strategic human resource management'. Available at: www.cipd.co.uk/knowledge/strategy/hr/strategic-hrm-factsheet#6744 (Accessed: January 2, 2019).

Clegg, H. (1979). *The System of Industrial Relations in Great Britain*. Oxford: Blackwell.

Coff, R. W. (1999). 'When competitive advantage doesn't lead to performance: The resource-based view and stakeholder bargaining power'. *Organization Science, 10*(2): 119–133.

Collins, C. J. & Clark, K. D. (2003). 'Strategic human resource practices, top management team social networks, and firm performance: The role of human resource practices in creating organizational competitive advantage'. *Academy of Management Journal, 46*(6): 740–751.

Collins, C. J. & Kehoe, R. R. (2009). 'Recruitment and selection'. In Storey, J., Wright, P. M. & Ulrich, D. (eds), *The Routledge Companion to Strategic Human Resource Management*. London and New York: Routledge.

Combs, J., Liu, Y., Hall, A. & Ketchen, D. (2006). 'How much do high-performance work practices matter? A meta-analysis of their effects on organizational performance'. *Personnel Psychology, 59*(3): 501–528.

Connelly, B. L., Certo, S. T., Ireland, R. D. & Reutzel, C. R. (2011). 'Signaling theory: a review and assessment'. *Journal of Management, 37*(1): 39–67.

Conway, E., Fu, N., Monks, K., Alfes, K. & Bailey, C. (2016). 'Demands or resources? The relationship between HR practices, employee engagement, and emotional exhaustion within a hybrid model of employment relations'. *Human Resource Management*, 55(5): 901–917.

Cook, H., MacKenzie, R. & Forde, C. (2016). 'HRM and performance: The vulnerability of soft HRM practices during recession and retrenchment'. *Human Resource Management Journal*, 26(4): 557–571.

Cowling, A. & Walters, M. (1990). 'Manpower planning: Where are we today?' *Personnel Review*, 19(3): 3–8.

Davenport, T. & Prusak, L. (1998). *Working Knowledge: How Organizations Manage What They Know*. Boston, MA: Harvard Business School Press.

Davenport, T., Leibold, M. & Voelpel, F. C. (2006). *Strategic Management in the Innovation Economy*. New York: Wiley.

Dawson, J. & West, M. (2018). *Employee Engagement, Sickness Absence and Agency Spend in NHS*. London: NHS England and The King's Fund.

DBEIS (2022) Trade union membership UK: Statistical Bulletin, Department for Business, Energy & Industrial Strategy, 25 May 2022.

De Vos, A. & Bart Cambré, B. (2017). 'Career management in high-performing organizations: A set-theoretic approach'. *Human Resource Management Journal*, 56(3): 501–518.

Deery, S., Rayton, B., Walsh, J. & Kinnie, N. (2017). 'The costs of exhibiting organizational citizenship behavior'. *Human Resource Management Journal*, 56(6): 1039–1049.

Delery, J. E. & Doty, D. H. (1996). 'Modes of theorizing in strategic human resource management: Tests of universalistic, contingency, and configurational performance predictions'. *Academy of Management Journal*, 39(4): 802–835.

Delery, J. E. & Shaw, J. D. (2001). 'The strategic management of people in work organizations: Review, synthesis, and extension'. *Research in Personnel and Human Resource Management*, 20: 165–197.

Delfanti, A. (2022) The Warehouse: Workers and Robot at Amazon, London: Pluto Press.

Deloitte (2011). *Business Driven HR: Unlock the Value of HR Business Partners*. London: Deloitte. Available at: www2.deloitte.com/content/dam/Deloitte/ie/Documents/People/Unlocking_the_value_of_HR_Business_Partners_High_Res.pdf (Accessed: January 2, 2019).

Di Pietro, F., Monaghan, S. & O'Hagan-Luff, M. (2022). 'Entrepreneurial Finance and HRM Practices in Small Firms', *British Journal of Management*, 33: 327–345

Doellgast, V., Bidwell, M. & Colvin, J. S. (2021). 'New directions in employment relations theory: Understanding fragmentation, identity and legitimacy'. *Industrial & Labor Relations Review*, 74(3): 555–579

Doeringer, P. B. & Piore, M. J. (1975). *Internal Labor Markets and Manpower Analysis*. New York: Heath Lexington.

Dumont, J., Shen, J. & Deng, X. (2019). 'Effects of green HRM practices on employee workplace green behavior: The role of psychological green climate and employee green values' *Human Resource Management*, 56(4): 613–627.

Dundon, T. & Rafferty, A. (2018). 'The (potential) demise of HRM?' *Human Resource Management Journal*, 28(3): 377–391.

Dunlop, J. T. (1958). *Industrial Relations Systems*. New York: Henry Holt.

Dyer, L. (1985). 'Strategic human resources management and planning'. *Research in Personnel and Human Resource Management*, *3*(1): 30.

Easterby-Smith, M., Lyles M. A. & Peteraf, M. A. (2009). 'Dynamic capabilities: Current debates and future directions'. *British Journal of Management*, *20*(Special Issue): S1–S8.

Edwards, R. (1979). *Contested Terrain: The Transformation of the Workplace in the Twentieth Century*. London: Heinemann.

Ehrnrooth, M., Barner-Rasmussen, W., Koveshnikov, A. & Tornroos, M. (2021). 'A new look at the relationships between transformational leadership and employee attitudes: Does a high-performance work system substitute and/or enhance these relationships?' *Human Resource Management*, *60*: 377–398.

Eisenberger, R., Huntington, R., Hutchison, S. & Sowa, D. (1986). 'Perceived organizational support'. *Journal of Applied Psychology*, *71*: 500–507.

Eisenhardt, K. M. & Martin, J. A. (2000). 'Dynamic capabilities: What are they?' *Strategic Management Journal*, *21*: 1105–1121.

Eurofound (2022). *Living and Working in Europe, Luxembourg. Publications Office of the European Union*. https://www.eurofound.europa.eu/data/covid-19

Farndale, E., Bonache, J., McDonnell, A. & Kwon, B. (2023). 'Positioning context front and center in international human resource management research'. *Human Resource Management Journal*, *33*(1): 1–16.

Felstead, A. & Reuschke, D. (2021). 'A flash in the pan or a permanent change? The growth of homeworking during the pandemic and its effect on employee productivity in the UK'. *Information Technology & People*, 10.1108/ITP-11-202 0-0758

Fitz-Enz, J. (2009). *The ROI of Human Capital*. New York: AMACOM.

Fitz-Enz, J. (2010). *The New HR Analytics*. New York: AMACOM.

Flanagan, F. (2017). 'Symposium on work in the gig economy'. *The Economic and Labour Relations Review*, *28*(3): 378–381.

Flanders, A. (1964). *The Fawley Productivity Agreements*. London: Faber.

Flanders, A. (1970). *Managers and Unions: The Theory and Reform of Industrial Relations*. London: Faber.

Fombrun, C. J., Tichy, N. M. & Devanna, M. A. (1984). *Strategic Human Resource Management*. New York: Wiley.

Fox, A. (1974). *Beyond Contract: Work, Power and Trust Relations*. London: Faber.

Gahan, P., Theilacker, M., Adamovic, M., Choi, D., Harley, B., Healy, J. & Olsen, J. E. (2021). 'Between fit and flexibility? The benefits of high-performance work practices and leadership capability for innovation outcomes', *Human Resource Management Journal*, *31*(2): 414–437.

Garavan, T., Ullah, I., O'Brien, F., Darcy C., Wisetsri, W., Afshan, G. & Mugha, Y. H. (2022). 'Employee perceptions of individual green HRM practices and voluntary green work behaviour: A signalling theory perspective'. *Asia Pacific Journal of Human Resource Management*, doi: 10.1111/1744-7941.12342

Gardner, T., Wright, P. M. & Moynihan, T. M. (2011). 'The impact of motivation, empowerment, and skill-enhancing practices on aggregate voluntary turnover: The mediating effect of collective affective commitment'. *Personnel Psychology*, *64*(2): 315–350.

Gerhart, B. (2007). 'Modeling HRM and performance linkages'. In Boxall, P., Purcell, J. & Wright, P. M. (eds), *The Oxford Handbook of Human Resource Management*. Oxford: Oxford University Press.

Gerhart, B. (2009). 'Compensation'. In Storey, J., Wright, P. M. & Ulrich, D. (eds), *The Routledge Companion to Strategic Human Resource Management*. London and New York: Routledge.

Gerhart, B. & Fang, M. (2005). 'National culture and human resource management: Assumptions and evidence'. *International Journal of Human Resource Management*, *16*(6): 971–986.

Gerhart, B., Wright, P. M. & McMahan, G. (2000). 'Measurement error in research on the human resources and firm performance relationship: Further evidence and analysis'. *Personnel Psychology*, *53*: 855–872.

Gerhart, B., Wright, P. M., McMahan, G. C. & Snell, S. A. (2000). 'Measurement error in research on human resources and firm performance: How much error is there and how does it influence effect size estimates?' *Personnel Psychology*, *53*(4): 803–834.

Gibson, C. B. & Birkinshaw, J. (2004). 'The antecedents, consequences, and mediating role of organizational ambidexterity'. *Academy of Management Journal*, *47*: 209–226.

Giles, W. F. & Findley, H. M. (1997). 'Procedural fairness in performance appraisal'. *Journal of Business*, *11*: 493–506.

Giudice, M. D., Scuotto, V., Ballestra L. V. & Pironti, M. (2022). 'Humanoid robot adoption and labour productivity: A perspective on ambidextrous product innovation routines'. *The International Journal of Human Resource Management*, *33*(6): 1098–1124

Glaister, A. J. (2014). 'HR outsourcing: The impact on HR role, competency development and relationships'. *Human Resource Management Journal*, *24*(2): 211–226.

Glaister, A. J., Karacay, G., Demirbag, M. & Tatoglu, E. (2018). 'HRM and performance: The role of talent management as a transmission mechanism in an emerging market context'. *Human Resource Management Journal*, *28*: 146–166.

Gold, M. & Smith, C. (2022). *Where's the 'Human' in Human Resource Management? Managing Work in the 21st Century*. Bristol: Bristol University Press.

Graham, M., Lehdonvirta, V. & Wood, A. (2017). *The Risks and Rewards of Online Gig Work at the Global Margins*. Oxford: Oxford Internet Institute.

Grant, R. (1991). 'The resource-based theory of competitive advantage: Implications for strategy formation'. *California Management Review*, *34*(Spring): 114–135.

Greenhouse, S. (2009). *The Big Squeeze: Tough Times for the American Worker*. New York: Anchor Books.

Groen, B. C., Wilderom, P. M. & Wouters, M. J. F. (2017). 'High job performance through co-developing performance measures with employees'. *Human Resource Management*, *56*(1): 11–32.

Guest, D. & Bos-Nehles, A. (2014). 'HRM and performance: The role of effective implementation'. In Paauwe, J., Guest, D. E. & Wright, P. M. (eds), *HRM and Performance: Achievements and Challenges*. London: Wiley.

Guest, D. & MacKenzie-Davey, K. (1996). 'Don't write off the traditional career'. *People Management*, February: 22–25.

Guest, D. E. (2011). 'Human resource management and performance: Still searching for some answers'. *Human Resource Management Journal, 21*(1): 3–13.

Guest, D. E., Michie, J., Conway, N. & Sheehan, M. (2003). 'Human resource management and corporate performance in the UK'. *British Journal of Industrial Relations, 41*(2): 291–314.

Guest, D. E., Bos-Nehles, A. C., Paauwe, J. & Wright, P. (2013). 'HRM and performance: The role of effective implementation'. In Guest, D., Paauwe, J. & Wright, P. M. (eds), *HRM and Performance: Achievements and Challenges*, 79–96. Chichester, UK: Wiley-Blackwell.

Guest, D. E., Wright, P. & Paauwe, J. (eds) (2013). *HRM and Performance: Achievements and Challenges*. Hoboken, NJ: Wiley-Blackwell.

Guest, D. E., Sanders, K., Rodrigues R. & Oliveira, T. (2021). 'Signalling theory as a framework for analysing human resource management processes and integrating human resource attribution theories: A conceptual analysis and empirical exploration'. *Human Resource Management Journal, 31*(3): 796–818.

Guthridge, M., Komm, A. & Lawson, E. (2008). 'Making talent a strategic priority'. *McKinsey Quarterly, 1*: 49–59.

Haggerty, J. J. & Wright, P. M. (2010). 'Strong situations and firm performance: A proposed reconceptualization of the role of the HR function'. In Wilkinson, A., Bacon, N., Redman, T. & Snell, S. (eds), *The Sage Handbook of Human Resource Management*. London: Sage.

Hall, P. A. & Soskice, D. (2001). *Varieties of Capitalism: The Institutional Foundations of Comparative Advantage*. Oxford: Oxford University Press.

Hammonds, K. H. (2005) *Why We Hate HR*. Boston, MA: Fast Company.

Han, J. H., Kang, S., Oh, I. S., Kehoe, R. R. & Lepak, D. P. (2019). 'The goldilocks effect of strategic human resource management? Optimizing the benefits of a high-performance work system through the dual alignment of vertical and horizontal fit'. *Academy of Management Journal, 62*(5): 1388–1412.

Hao, Z. & Liden, R. C. (2011). 'Internships'. *Journal of Applied Psychology, 96*(1): 221–229.

Harris, C. Wright, P. & McMahan, G. (2018). 'The emergence of human capital: Roles of social capital and coordination that drive unit performance'. *Human Resource Management Journal*, doi: 10.1111/1748-8583.12212.

Haskel, J. & Westlake, S. (2018). *Capitalism Without Capital: The Rise of the Intangible Economy*. Princeton: Princeton University Press.

Hauff, S., Alewell, D. & Hansen, N. (2014). 'HRM systems between control and commitment: Occurrence, characteristics, and effects on HRM outcomes and firm performance'. *Human Resource Management Journal, 24*(4): 424–441.

Hauff, S., Alewell, D. & Hansen, N. K. (2017). 'HRM system strength and HRM target achievement: Toward a broader understanding of HRM processes'. *Human Resource Management, 56*(5): 715–729.

Helpman, E. (2018). *Globalization and Inequality*. Boston: Harvard University Press.

Hermans, M. & Ulrich, M. (2021). 'How symbolic human resource function actions affect the implementation of high-performance work practices: The mediating effect of influence on strategic decision-making'. *Human Resource Management Journal, 31*: 1063–1081.

Hodgson, D., Gleadle, P. & Storey, J. (2012). '"The ground beneath my feet": Projects, project management and the intensified control of R&D engineers'. *New Technology, Work & Employment*, *27*(3): 163–177.

Hofstede, G. (1993). 'Cultural constraints in management theories'. *Academy of Management Executive*, 7: 81–94, doi: 10.5465/ame.1993.9409142061.

Holland, P., Cooper, B. & Sheehan, C. (2017). 'Employee voice, supervisor support, and engagement: The mediating role of trust HRM'. *Human Resource Management*, *56*(6): 915–929.

Holley, N. (2016). 'Part 1: HR business partnering: Ulrich 20 years on'. *Changeboard*. *Available at*: www.changeboard.com/content/5508/part-1-hr-business-partnering-ulrich-20-years-on/ (Accessed: January 24, 2023).

Holzer, H. J., Lane, J. I. & Vilhuber, L. (2004). 'Escaping low earnings: The role of employer characteristics and changes'. *Industrial and Labor Relations Review*, *57*(4): 560–578.

Homans, G. (1961). *Social Behavior: Its Elementary Forms*. New York: Harcourt Brace.

Hong, Y., Jiang, Y., Liao, H. & Sturman, M. C. (2017). 'High performance work systems for service quality: Boundary conditions and influence processes'. *Human Resource Management*, *56*(4): 747–767.

Hu, J., Zheng, X., Tepper, B. J., Li, N., Liu, X. & Yu, J. (2022). 'The dark side of leader–member exchange: Observers' reactions when leaders target their teammates for abuse'. *Human Resource Management*, *61*(2): 199–213.

Huffman, A. H., Albritton, D., Matthews, R. A., Muse, L. A. & Howes, S. S. (2022). 'Managing furloughs: How furlough policy and perceptions of fairness impact turnover intentions over time'. *The International Journal of Human Resource Management*, *33*(14): 2801–2828.

Huselid, M. (1995). 'The impact of human resource management practices on turnover, productivity, and corporate financial performance'. *Academy of Management Journal*, *38*(3): 635–672.

Huselid, M. A. (2018). 'The science and practice of workforce analytics: Introduction to the *HRM* special issue'. *Human Resource Management*, 57: 679–684.

Huselid, M.A., and Becker BE. (2000). 'Comment on measurement error in research on human resources and firm performance: How much error is there and how does it influence effect size estimates?' *Personnel Psychology*, *53*(4): 835–854.

ILO (2021). *World Employment and Social Outlook Trends 2021*. Geneva: International Labour Organization.

Ichniowski, C. & Shaw, K. (1999). 'The effects of human resource management systems on economic performance'. *Management Science*, 45: 704–720.

Ichniowski, C., Shaw, K. & Prenushi, G. (1997). 'The effects of HRM practices on productivity: A study of steel finishing lines'. *American Economic Review*, *87*(3): 291–313.

Ignjatovic, M. & Svetlik, I. (2003). 'European HRM Clusters'. *EBS Review*, Fall: 25–39.

Ingham, J. & Ulrich, D. (2016). 'Building better HR departments'. *Strategic HR Review*, *15*(3): 129–136.

Jensen, M. C. & Meckling, W. (1976). 'Theory of the firm: Managerial behavior, agency costs and ownership structure'. *Journal of Financial Economics, 3*: 305–360.

Jiang, K., Lepak, D. P., Hu, J. & Baer, J. C. (2012). 'How does human resource management influence organizational outcomes? A meta-analytic investigation of mediating mechanisms'. *Academy of Management Journal, 55*(6): 1264–1294.

John, S. & Bjorkman, I. (2015). 'In the eyes of the beholder: The HRM capabilities of the HR function as perceived by managers and professionals'. *Human Resource Management Journal, 25*(4): 424–442.

Johnson, G. (2004). 'To outsource or not to outsource ... That is the question'. *Training, 41*: 26–29.

Junni, P., Sarala, R. M., Tarba, S. Y., Liu, Y. & Cooper, C. L. (2015). Guest Editors' 'Introduction: The role of human resources and organizational factors in ambidexterity'. *Human Resource Management, 54*(S1): 1–28.

Kalleberg, A. (2013). *Good Jobs, Bad Jobs: The Rise of Polarized and Precarious Employment Systems in the United States, 1970s–2000s.* New York: Russel Sage Foundation.

Kalleberg, A. (2018). *Precarious Lives: Job Insecurity and Well-Being in Rich Democracies.* Cambridge, UK: Polity Press.

Kang, S.-C., Oldroyd, J. B., Morris, S. & Kim, J. (2018). 'Reading the stars: Determining human capital's value in the hiring process'. *Human Resource Management, 57*: 55–64.

Karabarbounis, L. & Neiman, B. (2013). 'The global decline of the labor share'. *NBER Working* Paper No. 19136. Cambridge, MA: National Bureau of Economic Research.

Katou, A., Budhwar, P. & Patel, C. (2021). 'Line manager implementation and employee HR attributions mediating mechanisms in the HRM system – organizational performance relationship: A multilevel and multipath study'. *Human Resource Management Journal, 31*(3): 775–795.

Katz, L. F. & Krueger, A. B. (2016). *The Rise and Nature of Alternative Work Arrangements in the United States, 1995–2015.* Boston, MA: Harvard University.

Katz, L. F. & Krueger, A. B. (2017). 'The role of unemployment in the rise in alternative work arrangements'. *American Economic Review Papers and Proceedings, 107*(5): 388–392.

Kaufman, B. E. (2015). 'Evolution of strategic HRM as seen through two founding books: A 30th anniversary perspective on development of the field'. *Human Resource Management, 54*(3): 389–407.

Kaufman, B. E. (2020). 'The real problem: The deadly combination of psychologization, scientism and normative promotionalism takes strategicg human resource management down a 30-year dead end', *Human Resource Management Journal, 30*(4): 49–72.

Kaufman, B. E. & Miller, B. I. (2011). 'The firm's choice of HRM practices: Economics meets strategic human resource management'. *Industrial and Labor Relations Review, 64*(3): 526–557.

Keegan, A. & Meijerink, J. (2023). 'Dynamism and realignment in the HR architecture: Online labor platform ecosystems and the key role of contractors'. *Human Resource Management, 62*(1), 15–29

Kellner, A., Townsend, K., Loudoun, R. & Wilkinson, R. (2023). 'High reliability Human Resource Management (HRM): A system for high risk workplaces'. *Human Resource Management Journal 33*(1): 170–186.

Kelly, J. & Gennard, J. (2007). 'Business strategic decision making: The role and influence of directors'. *Human Resource Management Journal, 17*(2): 99–117.

Ketchen, D. J., Crook, T. R., Todd, S. Y., Combs, J. G. & Woehr, D. J. (2015). 'Managing human capital: A meta-analysis of links among human resource practices and systems, human capital, and performance'. In Hitt, M. A., Jackson, S. E., Carmona, S., Bierman, L., Shaley C., & Wright, P. M. (eds), *The Oxford Handbook of Strategy Implementation*. New York: Oxford University Press.

Ketkar, S. & Sett, P. K. (2009). 'HR flexibility and firm performance: Analysis of a multi-level causal model'. *The International Journal of Human Resource Management, 20*(5): 1009–1038.

Ketkar, S. & Sett, P. K. (2010). 'Environmental dynamism, human resource flexibility, and firm performance: Analysis of a multi-level causal model'. *The International Journal of Human Resource Management, 21*(8): 1173–1206.

Khurana, R. (2002). 'The curse of the 'superstar' CEO'. *Harvard Business Review*, September: 3–8.

Kilroy, S., Flood, P. C., Bosak, J. & Chênevert, D. (2017). 'Perceptions of high-involvement work practices, person-organization fit, and burnout: A time-lagged study of health care employees'. *Human Resource Management, 56*(5): 821–835.

Kim, K., Ok, C., Kang, S-C, Bae, J. & Kwon, K. (2021). 'High-performance work systems with internal and external contingencies: The moderating roles of organizational slack and industry instability'. *Human Resource Management, 60*(3): 415–433

Kirkpatrick, I. & Hoque, K. (2022). 'Human resource professionals and the adoption and effectiveness of high-performance work practices'. *Human Resource Management Journal, 32*(2): 261–282.

Klein, H. J., Brinsfield, C. T. & Cooper, J. T. (2021). 'The experience of commitment in the contemporary workplace: An exploratory re-examination of commitment model antecedents'. *Human Resource Management, 60*: 885–902

Kluger, A. N. & DeNisi, A. (1998). 'Feedback interventions: Towards understanding of a double-edged sword'. *Current Directions in Psychological Science*, 7: 67–72.

Kochan, T. & Barocci, T. (1985). *Human Resource Management and Industrial Relations*. Boston, MA: Little Brown.

Kochan, T. & Osterman, P. (1994). *The Mutual Gains Enterprise*. Boston, MA: Harvard Business School Press.

Kochan, T., Katz, H. & McKersie, R. (1986). *The Transformation of American Industrial Relations*. New York: Basic Books.

Kochan, T. A., Katz, H. C. & McKersie, R. B. (2016). 'Updating The Transformation of American Industrial Relations. *Industrial & Labor Relations Review, 29*(5):1281–1284

Kruse, D. L. (1993). *Profit Sharing: Does it Make a Difference?* Kalamazoo, MI: Upjohn Institute.

Kruse, D. L., Freeman, R. B. & Blasi, R. J. (eds) (2010). Shared capitalism at work: Employee ownership. *Profit and Gain Sharing, and Broad-Based Stock Options*. Chicago, IL: University of Chicago Press.

Kryscynski, D. & Ulrich, D. (2015). 'Making strategic human capital relevant: A time-sensitive opportunity'. *Academy of Management Perspectives, 29*: 357–369.

Kryscynski, D., Reeves, C., Stice-Lusvardi, R., Ulrich, M. & Russell, G. (2018). 'Analytical abilities and the performance of HR professionals'. *Human Resource Management, 57*(3): 715–738.

Kuvandikov, A., Pendleton, A. & M. Goergen (2022). 'The impact of activist hedge funds on post-merger downsizing and performance', *British Journal of Management, 33*(1): 346–368.

Lado, A. A. & Wilson, M. C. (1994). 'Human resource systems and sustained competitive advantage: A competency-based perspective'. *Academy of Management Review, 19*(4): 699–727.

Lahteenmaki, S., Storey, J. & Vanhala, S. (1986). 'HRM and company performance: The use of measurement and the influence of economic cycles'. *Human Resource Management Journal, 8*(2): 51–65.

Langevin-Heavey, A., Beijer, S. E., Federman, J., Hermans, M., Klein, F., Mcclean, E. & Martinson, B. (2013). 'Measurement of human resource practices: Issues regarding scale, scope, source and substantive content'. In Paauwe, J., Guest, D. E. & Wright, P. M. (eds), *HRM and Performance: Achievements and Challenges*, 129–148. London: Wiley.

Lawler, E., Ulrich, D., Fitz-enz, J., Madden, J. & Maruca. R. (2004). *Human Resources Business Process Outsourcing: Transforming How HR Work Gets Done*. San Francisco, CA: Josey Bass.

Lawler, E. E. III (2005). 'From human resource management to organization effectiveness'. *Human Resource Management, 44*(2): 699–727.

Lawler, E. E. III & Boudreau, J. W. (2009). *Achieving Excellence in Human Resources Management: An Assessment of Human Resource Functions*. Stanford, CA: Stanford University Press.

Lawler, E. E. III & Boudreau, J. W. (2012). *Effective Human Resource Management: A Global Analysis*. Stanford, CA: Stanford University Press.

Lawler E. E. III & Boudreau J. W. (2015). *Global Trends in Human Resource Management: A Twenty-Year Analysis*. Redwood City, CA: Stanford University Press.

Lazear, E. P. (2000). 'Performance pay and productivity'. *American Economic Review, 90*: 1346–1361.

Lengnick-Hall, C. & Lengnick-Hall, M. (1988). 'Strategic human resource management: A review of the literature and a proposed typology'. *Academy of Manageemnt Review, 13*(3): 454–470.

Lengnick-Hall, C. A. & Lengnick-Hall, M. L. (1988). 'Strategic human resources management: A review of the literature and a proposed typology'. *Academy of Management Review, 13*(3): 454–470.

Lengnick-Hall, M. L., Lengnick-Hall, C. A., Andrade, L. S. & Drake, B. (2009). 'Strategic human resource management: The evolution of the field'. *Human Resource Management Review, 19*: 64–85.

Lepak, D. A. & Snell, S. A. (2003). *Managing the Human Resource Architecture for Knowledge-based competition*. San Francisco. CA: Jossey Bass.

Lepak, D. P. & Snell, S. (1999). 'The human resource architecture: Towards a theory of human capital allocation and development'. *Academy of Management Review*, *24*: 31–48.

Lepak, D. P. & Snell, S. A. (2002). 'Examining the human resource architecture: The relationships among human capital, employment, and human resource configurations'. *Journal of Management*, *28*(4): 517–543.

Lepak, D. P., Takeuchi, R. & Snell, S. A. (2003). 'Employment flexibility and firm performance: Examining the interactive effects of employment mode, environmental dynamism and technological intensity'. *Journal of Management*, *29*: 681–703.

Lepak, D. P., Liao, H., Chung, Y. & Harden, E. E. (2006). 'A conceptual review of human resource management systems in strategic human resource management research'. *Research in Personnel and Human Resources Management*, *25*(1): 217–271.

Levinthal, D. & March, J. G. (1993). 'The myopia of learning'. *Strategic Management Journal*, *14*: 95–112.

Lindert, P. H. & Williamson, J. G. (2017). *Unequal Gains: American Growth and Inequality Since 1700*, Princeton, NJ: Princeton University Press.

Locke, E. & Latham, G. P. (1990). *A Theory of Goal Setting and Task Performance*. New York: Prentice Hall.

Locke, E. A. & Feren, D. B. (1980). 'The relative effectiveness of four methods of motivating employee performance'. In Duncan, K. D. (ed), *Changes in Working Life*. New York: Wiley.

London Assembly (2016). *The Hourglass Economy: An Analysis of London's Labour Market*. London: London Assembly Economy Committee.

London, M. & Mone, E. M. (2009). 'Strategic performance management: Issues and trends'. In Storey, J., Wright P. M. & Ulrich D. (eds), *The Routledge Companion to Strategic Human Resource Management*. London and New York: Routledge.

Luu, T. T. (2021). 'Can green creativity be fostered? Unfolding the roles of perceived green human resource management practices, dual mediation paths, and perceived environmentally-specific authentic leadership'. *The International Journal of Human Resource Management*, 10.1080/09585192.2021.1986107.

López-Cotarelo, J. (2018). 'Line managers and HRM: A managerial discretion perspective'. *Human Resource Management Journal*, *28*: 255–271.

Ma, X., Shu, R., & Zhong, G (2019). 'How customer-oriented companies breed HR flexibility and improved performance: evidence from business-to-customer companies in China', *Asia Pacific Journal of Human Resources*, *59*(2): 330–353.

Mabey, C. & Zhao, S. (2016). 'Managing five paradoxes of knowledge exchange in networked organizations: New priorities for HRM?' *Human Resource Management Journal*, *27*(1): 39–57.

MacDuffie, J. P. (1995). 'Human resource bundles and manufacturing performance: Organisational logic and flexible production systems in the world auto industry'. *Industrial and Labor Relations Review*, *48*(2): 197–221.

March, J. G. (1991). 'Exploration and exploitation in organisational learning'. *Organisation Science*, *2*(1): 71–87.

March, J. G. & Simon, H. A. (1958). *Organizations*. New York: Wiley.

Marginson, P., Armstrong, P., Edwards, P. & Purcell, J. (1995). 'Managing labour in the global corporation: A survey-based analysis of multinationals operating in the UK'. *International Journal of Human Resource Management, 6*(3): 702–719.

Mayo, A. (1991). *Managing Careers.* London: Institute of Personnel Management.

Mayo, E. (1949). *The Social Problems of an Industrial Civilization.* London: Routledge.

McIver, D., Lengnick-Hall, C. A., Lengnick-Hall, M. L. & Ramachandran, I. (2013). 'Understanding work and knowledge management from a knowledge-in-practice perspective'. *Academy of Management Review, 38*(4): 597–620.

McKinsey Global Survey (2020). 'How COVID-19 has pushed companies over the technology tipping point-and transformed business forever', https://www.mckinsey.com/business-functions/strategy-and-corporate-finance/our-insights/how-covid-19-has-pushed-companies-over-the-technology-tipping-point-and-transformed-business-forever', New York: McKinsey & Company. Accessed 1st February 2023.

McLagan, P. A. & Bedrick, D. (1983). 'Models for excellence: The results of the ASTD training and development competency study'. *Training and Development Journal, 37*(6): 10–20.

Meier-Barthold, M., Biemann, T. & Alfes, K. (2022). 'Strong signals in HR management: How the configuration and strength of an HR system explain the variability in HR attributions'. *Human Resource Management*, 1–18. 10.1002/hrm.22146

Messersmith, J. G., Patel, P. C., Lepak, D. P. & Gould-Williams, J. S. (2011). 'Unlocking the black box: Exploring the link between high-performance work systems and performance'. *Journal of Applied Psychology, 96*(6): 1105.

Meuer, J. (2017). 'Exploring the complementarities within high-performance work systems: A set-theoretic analysis of UK firms'. *Human Resource Management, 56*(5): 651–672.

Milanovic, B. (2018). *Global Inequality: A New Approach for the Age of Globalization.* Boston: Harvard University Press.

Miles, R. & Snow, C. C. (1994). *Fit, Failure and the Hall of Fame: How Companies Succeed or Fail.* New York: Free Press.

Miles, R. E. & Snow, C. C. (1978). *Organizational Strategy, Structure, and Process.* New York: McGraw-Hill.

Miles, R. E. & Snow, C. C. (1985). 'Designing strategic human resources systems'. *Organizational Dynamics*, Summer: 36–52.

Miles, R. E. & Snow, C. C. (1986). 'Organizations: New concepts for new forms'. *California Management Review, 28*(3): 62–73.

Milliman, J., Von Glinow, M. & Nathan, M. (1991). 'Organizational life cycles and international human resource management in multinational companies. Implications for congruence theory'. *Academy of Management Review, 16*(2): 318–339.

Mintzberg, H. (1978). 'Patterns in strategy formation'. *Management Science, 24*(9): 934–948.

Mintzberg, H. & Lampel, J. (1999). 'Reflecting on the strategy process'. *Sloan Management Review*, Spring: 21–30.

Mintzberg, H., Ahlstrand, B. & Lampel, J. (1998). *Strategy Safari*. New York: The Free Press.

Mitchell, C. M. & Murray, J. C. (2017). *The Changing Workplaces Review: An Agenda for Workplace Rights*. Ontario: Ministry of Labour.

Nahapiet, J. & Ghoshal, S. (1998). 'Social capital, intellectual capital and the organizational advantage'. *Academy of Management Review*, *23*(2): 242–266.

Ngo, H. Y. & Loi, R. (2008). 'Human resource flexibility, organizational culture and firm performance: An investigation of multinational firms in Hong Kong'. *The International Journal of Human Resource Management*, *19*(9): 1654–1666.

Nishii, L. & Wright, P. (2008). 'Variability at multiple levels of analysis: Implications for strategic human resource management'. In Smith, D. B. (ed.), *The People Make the Place*. Mahwah, NJ: Lawrence Erlbaum Associates.

Nishii, L. H., Lepak, D. P. & Schneider, B. (2008). 'Employee attributions of the "why" of HR practices: Their effects on employee attitudes and behaviors, and customer satisfaction'. *Personnel Psychology*, *61*(3): 503–545.

Noe, R. A. & Tews, M. J. (2009). 'Strategic training and development'. In Storey, J., Wright, P. M. & Ulrich, D. (eds), *The Routledge Companion to Strategic Human Resource Management*. London and New York: Routledge.

Nonaka, I. & Takeuchi, H. (1995). *The Knowledge-Creating Company: How Japanese Companies Create the Dynamics of Innovation*. Oxford: Oxford University Press.

Noon, M. & Ogbonna E. (2021). 'Controlling management to deliver diversity and inclusion: Prospects and limits'. *Human Resource Management Journal*, *31*(4): 619–638.

Olsen, K. M., Sverdrup, T., Nesheim, T. & Kalleberg, A. L. (2016). 'Multiple foci of commitment in a professional service firm: Balancing complex employment relations'. *Human Resource Management Journal*, *26*(4): 390–407.

Osterman, P. (2017). *Who Will Care for Us? Long-Term Care and the Long-Term Workforce*. New York: Russell Sage Foundation.

Osterman, P. (2018). 'In search of the high road: Meaning and evidence'. *International Labor Review*, *71*(1): 3–34.

Paauwe, J. & Farndale, E. (2017). *Strategy, HRM, and Performance: A Contextual Approach*. Oxford: Oxford University Press.

Patel, C., Budhwar, P., Witzemann, A. & Katou, A. (2019). 'HR outsourcing: The impact on HR's strategic role and remaining in-house HR function'. *Journal of Business Research*, *103*, 397–406. doi: 10.1016/j.jbusres.2019.11.007. Available at: www.researchgate.net/publication/321215412_HR_outsourcing_The_impact_on_HR%27s_strategic_role_and_remaining_in-house_HR_function (Accessed: January 2, 2018).

Patel, P. C., Messersmith, J. G. & Lepak, D. P. (2013). 'Walking the tightrope: An assessment of the relationship between high-performance work systems and organizational ambidexterity'. *Academy of Management Journal*, *56*(5): 1420–1442.

Paulet, R., Holland, P. & Morgan, D. (2021). 'A meta-review of 10 years of green human resource management: Is Green HRM headed towards a roadblock or a revitalisation?'. *Asia Pacific Journal of Human Resources*, *59*(2): 159–183.

Pernkopf, K., Latzke M. & Mayrhofer W. (2021) 'Effects of mixed signals on employer attractiveness: A mixed-method study based on signalling and convention theory'. *Human Resource Management Journal*, *31*(2): 392–413.

Peteraf, M. A. (1993). 'The cornerstone of competitive advantage: A resource-based view'. *Strategic Management Journal, 14*: 179–191.

Peters, T. & Waterman, R. (1982). *In Search of Excellence*. New York: Harper & Row.

Pfeffer, J. (1994). *Competitive Advantage Through People*. Boston, MA: Harvard University Press.

Pham, D. D. T. & Paille, P. (2019). 'Green recruitment and selection: An insight into green patterns'. *International Journal of Manpower, 41*(3): 258–272.

Piketty, T. (2014). *Capital in the 21st Century*. Boston, MA: Harvard University Press.

Piore, M. & Schrank, A. (2018). *Root Cause Regulation: Protecting Work and Workers in the Twenty First Century*. Boston, MA: Harvard University Press.

Polanyi, M. (1966). *The Tacit Dimension*. Chicago, IL: University of Chicago Press.

Porter, M. E. (1980). *Competitive Strategy*. New York: Free Press.

Posthuma, R. A., Campion, M. C., Masimova, M. & Campion, M. A. (2013). 'A high performance work practices taxonomy integrating the literature and directing future research'. *Journal of Management, 39*(5): 1184–1220.

Prahalad, C. K. & Hamel, G. (1990). 'The core competence of the corporation'. *Harvard Business Review, 68*: 79–88.

Pudil, P., Komarkova, L., Mikova, I. & Pribyl, V. (2018). 'Empirical study of screening and signalling theory in HRM'. *European Conference on Management, Leadership & Governance*, p. 231-XII.

Purcell, J. (2014). 'Disengaging from engagement'. *Human Resource Management Journal, 25*(3): 241–254.

Quade, M. J., Bonner, J. M., & Greenbaum, R. L. (2020). 'Management without morals: Construct development and initial testing of amoral management'. *Human Relations. 75*(2): 273–303. 10.1177/0018726720972784

Quinn, J. B. (1992). *Intelligent Enterprise*. New York: Free Press.

Rabl, T., Jayasinghe, M., Gerhart, B. & Kuhlmann, T. (2014). 'A meta-analysis of country differences in the high-performance work system–business perform-ance relationship: The roles of national culture and managerial discretion'. *Journal of Applied Psychology, 99*(6): 1011–1041.

Rasmussen, T. & Ulrich, D. (2015). 'Learning from practice: How HR analytics avoids becoming a fad'. *Organizational Dynamics, 44*(3): 236–242.

Ready, D. A., Conger, J. A. & Hill, L. A. (2010). 'Are you a high potential?' *Harvard Business Review, 88*(6): 78–84.

Ren, S., Jiang, K. & Tang, G. (2022). 'Leveraging green HRM for firm per-formance: The joint effects of CEO environmental belief and external pollution severity and the mediating role of employee environmental commitment'. *Human Resource Management, 61*(1): 75–90

Roebuck, C. (2015). 'What follows after Ulrich's business partner model?' *HR Gazette*. Available at: http://hr-gazette.com/what-follows-after-ulrichs-business-partner-model/ (Accessed: January 2, 2019).

Rossman, J. (2021). *The Amazon Way*, 3rd edition. New York: Clyde Hill Publishing.

Roundy, P. T. & Burke-Smalley, L. (2022). 'Leveraging entrepreneurial ecosys-tems as human resource systems: A theory of metaorganizational human resource management'. *Human Resource Management Review, 32*(4), 100863

Rubery, J., Earnshaw, J. & Marchington, M. (2002). 'Changing organisational forms and the employment relationship'. *Journal of Management Studies*, *39*(5): 645–672.

Russo, S. D., Miraglia, M. & Borgogni, L. (2017). 'Reducing organizational politics in performance appraisal: The role of coaching leaders for age-diverse employees'. *Human Resource Management Journal*, *56*(4): 769–783.

Sadun, R., Bloom, N. & Van Reenen, J. (2017). 'Why do we undervalue competent management?' *Harvard Business Review*, September-October: 121–127.

Salaman, G. & Storey, J. (2016). *A Better Way of Doing Business? Lessons from the John Lewis Partnership*. Oxford: Oxford University Press.

Salas-Vallina, A., Alegre, J. & Lopez-Cabrales (2021). 'The challenge of increasing employees' well-being and performance: How human resource management practices and engaging leadership work together toward reaching this goal'. *Human Resource Management*, *60*(3): 333–347.

Sanchez, R. (1995). 'Strategic flexibility in product competition'. *Strategic Management Journal*, *16*(S1): 135–159.

Sanders, K., Guest, D., & Rodrigues, R. (2021). 'The role of HR attributions in the HRM – Outcome relationship: Introduction to the special issue'. *Human Resource Management Journal*, *31*(3): 694–703.

Sanders, K., Bednall, T. C. & Yang, H. (2021). 'HR strength: Past, current and future research'. In Sanders, K., Yang, H. & Patel, C. (eds), *Handbook on HR Process Research*, 27–45. Edward Elgar Publishing. 10.4337/97818391 00079.00010

Schepker, D. J., Kim, Y., Patel, P. C. & Campion, M. C. (2017). *Leadership Quarterly*, *28*(6): 701–720.

Schmidt, J., Pohler, D. & Willness, C. R. (2017). 'Strategic HR system differentiation between jobs: The effects on firm performance and employee outcomes'. *Human Resource Management*, *57*(1): 65–81.

Schuler, R. & Jackson, S. (1987). 'Linking competitive strategies with human resource management practices'. *Academy of Management Executive*, *1*(3): 207–219.

Schuler, R., Jackson, S. & Jiang, K. (2014). 'An aspirational framework for strategic human resource management'. *Academy of Management Annals*, *8*: 1–56.

Schuler, R. S., Jackson, S. E. & Storey, J. (2001). 'HRM and its link with strategic management'. In Storey, J. (ed), *Human Resource Management: A Critical Text*, 114–130. London: Thomson Learning.

Scott-Jackson, W. & Mayo, A. (2017). *HR with Purpose: Future Models of HR*. Available at: www.henley.ac.uk/hrc (Accessed: January 2, 2019).

Shipton, H., Sparrow, P., Budhwar, P. & Brown, A. (2016). 'HRM and innovation: Looking across levels'. *Human Resource Management Journal*, *27*(2): 246–263.

Shuck, B., Adelson, J. & Reio, T. G. (2017). 'The employee engagement scale: Initial evidence for construct validity and implications for theory and practice'. *Human Resource Management*, *56*(6): 953–977.

Sisson, K. (1995). 'Human resource management and the personnel function'. In Storey, J. (ed), *Human Resource Management: A Critical Text*. London: Routledge.

Sisson, K. (2001). 'Human resource management and the personnel function: A case of partial impact?' In Storey, J. (ed), *Human Resource Management: A Critical Text* (2nd edition). London: Thomson.

Snell, S. A. (1992). 'Control theory in strategic human resource management: The mediating effect of administrative information'. *Academy of Management Journal, 35*(2): 292–327.

Snell, S. A. & Dean, J. W. (1992). 'Integrated manufacturing and human resource management: A human capital perspective'. *Academy of Management Journal, 35*(3): 467–504.

Snell, S. A., Swart, J., Morris, S. & Boon, C. (2023). 'The HR ecosystem: Emerging trends and a future research agenda', *Human Resource Management, 62*(1): 5–14.

Snow, C. C. (1992). 'Managing 21st century network organizations'. *Organizational Strategy, 16*(4): 38–42.

Sparrow, P. & Makram, H. (2015). 'What is the value of talent management?: Building value-driven processes within a talent management architecture'. *Human Resource Management Review, 25*(3): 249–263.

Srikant, C., Pichler, S. & Shafiq, A. (2021). 'The virtuous cycle of diversity'. *Human Resource Management, 60*(4): 535–558

Standing, G. (2011). *The Precariat: The New Dangerous Class.* London: Bloomsbury Academic.

Stanford, J. (2017). 'The resurgence of gig work: Historical and theoretical perspectives'. *The Economic and Labour Relations Review, 28*(3): 382–401.

Stirpe, L., Trullen, J. & Bonache, J. (2013). 'Factors helping the HR function gain greater acceptance for its proposals and innovations: Evidence from Spain'. *The International Journal of Human Resource Management, 24*(20): 3794–3811.

Storey, J. (1992). *Developments in the Management of Human Resources.* Oxford: Blackwell.

Storey, J. (1998) 'Beyond organizational structure: The end of classical forms?'. In Mabey, C., Salaman, G. & Storey, J. (eds), *Human Resource Management: A Strategic Introduction*, 253–274. Oxford: Blackwell.

Storey, J. (ed) (2007). *Human Resource Management: A Critical Text* (3rd edition). London: Thomson.

Storey, J. & Sisson, K. (1993). *Managing Human Resources and Industrial Relations.* Buckingham, UK: Open University Press.

Su, Z. X. & Wright, P. M. (2012). 'The effective human resource management system in transitional China: A hybrid of commitment and control practices'. *The International Journal of Human Resource Management, 23*(10): 2065–2086.

Su, Z. X., Wright, P. M. & Ulrich, M. D. (2018). 'Going Beyond the SHRM paradigm examining four approaches to governing employees,' *Journal of Management, 24*(4): 1598–1619.

Sun, L-Y, Aryee, S. & Law, K. S. (2007). 'High-performance human resource practices, citizenship behaviour and organizational performance: A relational perspective'. *Academy of Management Journal, 50*(3): 558–577.

Takeuchi, R., Lepak, D. P., Wang, H. & Takeuchi, K. (2007). 'An empirical examination of the mechanisms mediating between high-performance work systems and the performance of Japanese organizations'. *Journal of Applied Psychology, 92*(4): 1069.

Tannenbaum, S. & Woods, S. (1992). 'Determining a strategy for evaluating training'. *Human Resource Planning, 15*: 63–81.

Tavis, A. (2018). 'Talent management: The end of the era or the dawn of the new age?' People + Strategy. *Journal of the Human Resource Planning Association, 41*(1): 4.

Taylor, M. (2018). *Good Work: The Taylor Review of Modern Working Practices.* London: Department for Business, Energy and Industrial Strategy.

Taylor, S. & Storey, J. (2016). 'Strategic leadership development: The work of corporate universities'. In Storey, J. (ed), *Leadership in Organizations: Current Issues and Key Trends.* London: Routledge.

Teece, D. J., Pisano, G. & Shuen. A. (1997). 'Dynamic capabilities and strategic management'. *Strategic Management Journal, 18*(7): 509–533.

Thompson, J. D. (1967). *Organizations in Action.* New York: McGraw-Hill.

Troth, A. & Guest, D. (2020). 'The case for psychology in HRM'. *Human Resource Management Journal, 30*(4): 34–48.

Trullen, J., Stirpe, L., Bonache J. & Valverde M. (2016). 'The HR department's contribution to line managers' effective implementation of HR practices'. *Human Resource Management Journal, 26*(4): 449–470.

Truss, C. & Gratton, L. (1994). 'Strategic human resource management: A conceptual approach'. *International Journal of Human Resource Management, 5*: 663–686.

Truss, C., Delbridge, R., Alfes, K., Shantz, A. & Soane, E. (2014). 'Introduction'. In Truss, C., Delbridge, R., Alfes, K., Shantz, A. & Soanne, E. (eds), *Employee Engagement in Theory and Practice.* Abingdon, UK: Routledge.

Tsay, A. A., Gray, J. V., Noh, I. J. & Mahoney, J. T. (2018). 'Review of production and operations management research on outsourcing in supply chains: Implications for the theory of the firm'. *Production and Operations Management, 27*(7): 1177–1220.

Turner, L. A. & Merriman, K. K. (2022). 'Cultural intelligence and establishment of organisational diversity management practices: An upper echelons perspective'. *Human Resource Management Journal, 32*(2), 321–340

Tyson, S. & Fell, A. (1986). *Evaluating the Personnel Function.* London: Hutchinson.

Tzabbar, D., Tzafrir, S. & Baruch, Y. (2017). 'A Bridge Over Troubled Water: Replication, Integration and Extension of the Relationship between HRM Practices and Organizational Performance Using Moderating Meta-Analysis'. *Human Resource Management Review, 27*(1): 134–148.

Ulrich, D. (1997). *Human Resource Champions: The Next Agenda for Adding Value and Delivering Results.* Boston, MA: Harvard Business School Press.

Ulrich, D. (1998). 'A new mandate for human resources'. *Harvard Business Review, 76*(1): 124–134.

Ulrich, D. & Allen, J. (2017). 'PE firms are creating a new role: Leadership capital partner'. *Harvard Business Review.* August.

Ulrich, D. & Lake, D. G. (1990). *Organizational Capability: Competing from the Inside Out.* New York: John Wiley & Sons.

Ulrich, D., Brockbank, W. & Younger, J. (2008). 'The next evolution of the HR organization'. In Storey, J., Wright, P. & Ulrich, D. (eds), *Routledge Companion to Strategic Human Resource Management.* New York: Routledge.

Ulrich, D., Allen, J., Brockbank, W., Younger, J. & Nyman, M. (2009). *HR Transformation: Building Human Resources From the Outside In*. New York: McGraw-Hill.

Ulrich, D., Brockbank, W., Younger, J. & Ulrich, M. (2012). *Global HR Competencies: Mastering Competitive Value from the Outside-In*. New York: McGraw-Hill.

Ulrich, D. and Grochowski, J. (2012) 'From shared services to professional services', *Strategic HR Review*, *11*(3) 136–142.

Ulrich, D., Younger, J., Brockbank, W. & Ulrich, M. D. (2013). 'The state of the HR profession'. *Human Resource Management*, *52*(3): 457–471.

Ulrich, D., Kryscynski, D., Ulrich, M. & Brockbank, W. (2017). *Victory Through Organization: Why the War for Talent is Failing Your Company and What You Can Do About It*. New York: McGraw-Hill.

Van Wanrooy, B., Bewley H., Bryson A., Forth, J., Freeth, S. Stokes, L. & Wood, S. (2013). *Employment Relations in the Shadow of Recession: Findings from the 2011 Workplace Employment Relations Study*. Basingstoke, UK: Palgrave Macmillan.

Van den Groenendaal, S. M. E., Freese, C., Poell, R. F., Dorien, T. A. M. & Kooij, D. T. A. M. (2023). 'Inclusive human resource management in free-lancers' employment relationships: The role of organizational needs and free-lancers' psychological contracts.' *Human Resource Management Journal*, *33*(1) 224–240.

Venkatraman, N. (1989). 'The concept of fit in strategy research: Toward verbal and statistical correspondence'. *Academy of Management Review*, *14*(3): 423–444.

Viswesvaran, C., Ones, D. S. & Schmidt, F. (1996). 'Comparative analysis of the reliability of job performance ratings.' *Journal of Applied Psychology*. *81*(5): 557–574.

Wall Street Journal (2022). 'Google's Owner Paid $296,000 to a Typical Worker. Here's What Other Firms Pay'. *Wall Street Journal*, June 1st. https://www.wsj.com/articles/what-alphabet-meta-and-other-s-p-500-firms-paid-workers-last-year-11654084801.

Walton, R. E. (1985). 'From control to commitment in the workplace'. *Harvard Business Review*, *63*(2): 77–84.

Way, S. (2002). 'High performance work systems and intermediate indicators of firm performance within the US small business sector'. *Journal of Management*, *28*(6): 765–785.

Way, S. et al. (2015). 'Validation of a multidimensional HR flexibility measure'. *Journal of Management*, *41*(4): 1098–1131.

Way, S., Wright, P. M., Tracey, J. B. & Isnard, J. F. (2018). 'HR flexibility: Precursors and the contingent impact on firm financial performance'. *Human Resource Management*. *57*(2): 567–582.

Way, S., Ulrich, M. & Wright, P. (2023). *High-performance work systems, HR flexibility, organization size, and performance: The advantage of being large*. [Article under review].

Weick, K. (1979). *The Social Psychology of Organizing* (2nd edition). New York: McGraw-Hill.

Weil, D. (2014). *The Fissured Workplace: Why Work Became So Bad for So Many and What Can be Done to Improve it*. Boston: Harvard University Press.

Wernerfelt, B. (1984). 'A resource-based view of the firm'. *Strategic Management Journal*, *5*(2): 171–180.

World Economic Forum (2021). The Great Resignation https://www.weforum. org/agenda/2021/11/what-is-the-great-resignation-and-what-can-we-learn-from-it/ (accessed 1st Feb 2023).

Wright, P. & Nishii, L. (2013). 'Strategic HRM and organizational behavior: Integrating multiple levels of analysis'. In Guest, D., Paauwe, J. & Wright, P. (eds), *Human Resource Management and Performance: Building the Evidence Base*, 97–110. Oxford: Blackwell.

Wright, P., Nyberg, A., Schepker, D., Cragun, O. & Ulrich, M. (2016). *The Changing Chief Human Resources Officer Role: Results of the 2016 HR@Moore Survey of Chief HR Officers*. Columbia, SC: Center for Executive Succession, University of South Carolina.

Wright, P., Nyberg, A. & Ployhart, R. (2018). 'A research revolution in SHRM: New challenges and research directions'. In Buckley, M. (ed), *Research in Personnel and Human Resource Management*, 36: 141–163.

Wright, P. M. & Boswell, W. R. (2002). 'Desegregating HRM: A review and synthesis of micro and macro human resource management research'. *Journal of Management*, 28(3): 247–276.

Wright, P. M. & McMahan, G. C. (1992). 'Theoretical perspectives for strategic human resource management'. *Journal of Management*, 18(2): 295–320.

Wright, P. M. & McMahan, G. C. (2011). 'Exploring human capital: Putting "human" back into strategic human resource management'. *Human Resource Management Journal*, 21(2): 93–104.

Wright, P. M. & Nishii, L. H. (2006). 'Strategic HRM and organizational behavior: Integrating multiple levels of analysis'. *CAHRS Working Paper Series No. 06–05*. Ithaca, NY: Cornell University, School of Industrial and Labor Relations, Center for Advanced Human Resource Studies. Available at: http://digitalcommons.ilr.cornell.edu/cahrswp/405 (Accessed: January 2, 2019).

Wright, P. M. & Sherman, W. S. (1999). 'Failing to find fit in strategic human resource management: Theoretical and empirical problems'. *Research in Personnel and Human Resources Management*, 4: 53–74.

Wright, P. M. & Snell, S. A. (1998). 'Toward a unifying framework for exploring fit and flexibility in strategic human resource management'. *Academy of Management Review*, 23: 756–772.

Wright, P. M., McMahan, G. C. & McWilliams, A. (1994). 'Human resources and sustained competitive advantage: A resource-based perspective'. *International Journal of Human Resource Management*, 5(2): 301–326.

Wright, P. M., Gardner, T. M., Moynihan, L. M. & Allen, M. R. (2005). 'The relationship between HR practices and firm performance: Examining causal order'. *Personnel Psychology*, 58(2): 409–446.

Wright, P. M., Guest, D. & Paauwe, J. (2015). 'Off the mark: Response to Kaufman's evolution of strategic HRM'. *Human Resource Management*, 54(3): 409–415.

Youndt, M. A., Snell, S. A., Dean, J. W. & Lepak, D. P. (1996). 'Human resource management, manufacturing strategy, and firm performance'. *Academy of Management Journal*, 39(4): 836–866.

Zgola, M. (2021). 'Will the gig economy become the working-class norm?' *Forbes*, https://www.forbes.com/sites/forbesbusinesscouncil/2021/08/12/will-the-gig-economy-become-the-new-working-class-norm/ (Accessed 2nd Feb 2023).

Index

Note: page numbers in *italics* refer to figures.

ability, motivation, and opportunity (AMO) perspective 28
Academy of Management Journal 28
adaptation 82
adaptive capacity 82
administrative experts 56
advanced manufacturing technology 20
agency theory 67
agility 82–86
Akerlof, G. 59
Alfes, K. 24, 94
alignment 82, 90
alternative work arrangements 69
Amazon 64, 72
ambidexterity 76, 82, 84
American Society for Training and Development 52
analysers 18
analytics 59
analytics designer and interpreter 54, 74
angel investors 2
annual performance reviews 40
Apple 63
architects 49
Arrow, K. 59
Arthur, M. B. 20, 21, 79–80
artificial intelligence (AI) 72–73
automation 94
Autor, D. 68

Baird, L. 19, 80
Bad jobs 63
Barney, J. 19
Barocci, T. 15

Batt, R. 22, 71–73
Becker, B. 28, 30, 50, 79, 81
Behavioural Perspective 18, 79
Beltrán-Martin, I. 79, 81, 84, 85–86
best practices 9
Bhattacharya, M. 83, 84
Birkinshaw, J. 82
black box 22–23, 50, 93
Blair, T. 69
Bloodworth, J. 68
Bos-Nehles, A. C. 24
Boston Consulting Group and 52
Boudreau, J. 13
boundaryless career 37
Bowen, D. E. 23
Boyatzis, R. 52
Bryar, C. 72
bundling 28
business life-cycle, linking SHRM to 15
business partners 6, 56
business strategy: definition of 11; SRHM linking to 14–15
Butterick, M. 91
buy and build approaches 67

Caldwell, R. 49
call centres 22
Canada 94
capability 58
capitalism, varieties of 71
Cappelli, P. 22
career management 37
Carr, B. 72
centres of expertise 6, 56
Chadwick, C. 78

Chang, E. 93
Chang, S. 84
change agents 56
Changing Workplaces Review 69, 95
Chartered Institute of Personnel and
    Development (CIPD) 52
Chief Executive Officer (CEO) 96
Chief HR Officer (CHRO) 96
China, lockdowns in 2
Clark, K. D. 23
clerk of works 49
cluster organizations 45
Coase, R. 59
coherence 12
collective bargaining 5, 43, 62, 66
Collins, C. J. 23
Combs, J. 26, 27, 30
commitment maximisers 20
commitment-oriented practices 28
compensation 40–41
The Competent Manager (Boyatzis) 52
competitive advantage 5, 7, 11, 13, 14,
    19, 66
Competitive Advantage through People
    (Pfeffer) 62
complementary perspective 82–83
compliance manager 54
Connelly, B. L. 93
contingency models and frameworks
    14–17
contracts managers 49
coordinated market economies
    (CMEs) 71
coordination flexibility 83
cost-reducers 20
COVID-19 pandemic 1–2, 64
credible activist 53
cultural constraint hypothesis 27
culture 26–27
culture and change champion 53–54
cycle of HR practices *33*

de facto strategy 12
Dean, J. W. 20, 21
decision science 13
defenders 18
Delery, J. E. 21, 77, 79
Delfanti, A. 72
Deliveroo 70
Deloitte 52
design 13
deskilling 72
determinants 19–21

Di Pietro, F. 2, 68
digitalization 72–73, 89
disability 93
divisionalising 45–46
Doellgast, V. 5
Doty, D. H. 21, 77, 79
Du Pont 46
dual economy 63
Dyer, L. 23
dynamic capability 13

eco-systems 6
Ehrnrooth, M. 26
emergent strategy 12
employee attributions 24
employee champions 56
employee engagement 8, 43–45
employee experience 8
employee reactions, concept of 24
employee relations 4
employment engagement 43–45
employment management 4; High
    Road approach 8; Low Road
    approach 8
employment relations 43–45, 88–89
entrepreneurship 66–68
Equality, Diversity and Inclusion
    (EDI) 2, 16
equity financing 2
ESG 74
European Foundation for the
    Improvement of Living and
    Working Conditions 65
external fit 10

Facebook 88
*The Fall of the Labor Share and the
    Rise of Superstar Firms* (Autor
    et al.) 68
Fang, M. 26
Fell, A. 49
Felstead, A. 64
financialization 67, 90
financing, forms of 2
fissured workplace 69
fit 76–81; as covariation 77; as gestalts
    77, 79–80; as matching 77; as
    mediation 77, 79; as
    moderation 77–79, 81; as
    profile deviation 77, 79
flexibility 82–86
flexibility-oriented HRM systems
    (FHRM) 86

Fombrun, C. J. 15
four-task model 79
franchising 69
freelancers 14, 68
furloughs 64

gainsharing 41
Garavan, T. 93
Gardner, T. 28
General Motors 46
Gerhart, B. 26, 28, 81
Gibson, C. 82
gig economy 44, 68–69, 70, 95
globalization 42, 71–73, 75
Gold, M. 3
good practices 9
*Good Work: The Taylor Review of
    Modern Working Practices*
    (Taylor) 44, 69, 94–95
Google 63, 88
Grant, R. 11
Gratton, L. 23
Great Resignation 65
green HRM 73–74
Guest, D. E. 4, 24, 25, 29, 93

Haggerty, J. J. 50
Hall, P. A. 71
Hamel, G. 11
Hammonds, K. H. 50
Han, J. H. 78
hard and soft HRM 9
Harvard Business Review 92, 95
Harvard Model 5
Haskel, J. 63, 64
Hauff, S. 80
Hayek, F. 59
health and wellness management 43–45
hedge funds 2
Hewlett Packard 88
High Road approach 8, 90
High-Performance Work Practices 21
High-Performance Work Systems
    (HPWS) 3, 8, 22, 33, 78–79,
    81, 86, 91
high-performance working 88
High-Performance Workplaces
    theory 8
*Hired: Six Months Undercover in Low
    Wage Britain* (Bloodworth) 68
Hofstede, G. 26
homeworking 64
Hoque, K. 3

hourglass economy 9, 63
HR Analytics 59–60
HR competences 48–61; backstory
    49–51; defining 51–53;
    domains of 53–55; HR
    departments 55–60; key
    principles 52; Ulrich
    competency model 53–55, *54*
HR Context/Deliverables
    dimension 58
HR departments 55–60; dimensions of
    57, 57–58; power of
    organization effect 56; roles
    within 56; waves of HR value
    creation 59–60, *60*
HR design dimension 58
HR Magazine 92, 95
HR Practices 59
HR practices and performances: black
    box 22–23; bundling in,
    concept of 27; demonstrating
    relationships between 21–22;
    positive relationships 26–27;
    process models 21–22;
    value 30
HR Professionals 59
HR strategy dimension 58
HR theorizing 90–92
HR Work Style 59
human capital 5, 14
human capital curator 54
human capital management 4
Human Resource Champions
    (Ulrich) 56
human resource development (HRD)
    41–43
Human Resource Information Systems
    (HRIS) 36
human resource management (HRM):
    cultural, structural and
    personnel techniques 8–9;
    definition of 4, 7–8; ebb and
    flow of 66–71; green 73–74;
    nature of strategy in 10–11;
    theory and practice 9–10
human resource planning (HRP)
    34–37; idealized model of *35*
human resources 5
Huselid, M. A. 21, 28, 30, 50, 77, 79,
    80–81
Hyatt Regency Hotels 69
hypertext organizations 45
Hyun Chin, H. 93

Ignjatovic, M. 80
Implemented HR Practices 23
In Search of Excellence movement 46
income inequality 63
industrial relations 4
institutional complementarities
        theory 71
intangible assets 63
intangible economy 63
integrated manufacturing 20
interaction orientation 85
internal fit 10
International Labor Organisation 65
Islamic finance 2

Jackson, S. E. 14, 18
Jiang, K. 22, 28–29
John Lewis Partnership 2
just-in-time inventory control 20

Kalleberg, A. 94
Katou, A. 25, 85–86
Kaufman, B. E. 91
Ketkar, S. 83
Khurana, R. 34
Kim, K. 3
Kirkpatrick, I. 3
Klotz, A. 65
knowledge work 73
knowledge workers 42
Kochan, T. 15, 44
Kuvandikov, A. 68

labor unions 43–44, 65–66
Lado, A. A. 19
Langevin-Heavey, A. 28
Lawler, E. 50
LGBT+ 95
Lengnick-Hall, C. A. 19
Lengnick-Hall, M. L. 80
Lepak, D. P. 20, 36, 79, 80
leveraged buyouts 2
liberal market economies (LMEs) 71
Lindert, P. H. 63
Living and Working in Europe 2
lockdown laws 1
Loi, R. 83
Low Road approach 8, 88, 90

MacDuffie, J. P. 21, 27, 78
management practices 6, 88
manpower planning 36
McBer and Company 52

McClelland, D. 51–52
McMahan, G. 6, 76
Meier-Barthold, M. 94
Meshoulam, I. 19, 80
Miles, R. 18
Milliman, J. 82
Mintzberg, H, 12

National Organizations Survey 50
networks 45
Neumark, D. 22
neuroscience 3, 93
new normal 2
Ngo, H. Y. 83
Nishii, L. 24
Nobel Prize winners 59

online labour platforms (OLPs) 89
organization capability 58
organization design 45–46
organizational ambidexterity (OA) 82
organizational culture management
        45–47
organizational learning 43
organizational strategy and structure
        15–16
organizations 56
orthogonal perspective 82
Osterman, P. 94, 96
Ostroff, C. 23
outsourcing 35, 42, 46, 49, 51, 63, 69,
        72, 90

P&O Ferries 69
paradox navigator 53
Patel, P. C. 84
payment by results (PBR) 40
peer-to-peer lending 2
people management 4
performance: HR practices and 20;
        reward management and
        38–40
performance management 38–40
performance management systems *39*
performance outcomes 16–17, 18–31
performance-related pay (PRP) 40–41
Pernkopf, K. 93
personnel administration 4
personnel management 4
Pfeffer, J. 62
Planned HR Practices 23
plurality of interests 43
Porter, M. E. 43

portfolio careers 37
Posthuma, R. A. 43
power of organization effect 56
practice areas 32–47; compensation
    40–41; cycle of HR practices
    33; employment engagement
    43–45; employment relations
    43–45; health and wellness
    management 43–45; human
    resource development 41–43;
    human resource planning and
    resourcing 34–37; organization
    design 45–47; performance
    and reward management
    38–40; recruitment and
    selection 37–38; talent
    management 41–43
Prahalad, C. K. 11
precarious work 37, 63, 69, 88
private equity 67
process models 23, 94–95
productivity 6
productivity agreements 66
prospectors 18
Pudil, P. 93

quiet quitting 65

Rabl, T. 27
Ramstad, P. 13
recruitment 37–38
regulation 69–71
reputation 57–58
resource flexibility 83
resource-based theory (RBT) 19
resource-based view (RBV) 5, 11, 88
resourcing 34–37
Reuschke, D. 64
reward 38–40
role behaviours 18
Royal Dutch Shell 36

Salas-Vallina, A. 29
Sanchez, R. 83
Sanders, K. 24
Schuler, R. S. 14, 18, 23
selection 37–38
Sett, P. K. 83
shared services 6, 56
Shaw, J. D. 79
signalling theory 3, 93–94
Simon, S. 59
Sisson, K. 33, 49

skill development 42
skills gaps 75–87
Smith, C. 3
Snell, S. A. 20, 21, 36, 80, 82, 83, 84
Snow, C. C. 18
social exchange theory 18
social purpose 16–17
sorting effect 41
Soskice, D. 71
Spence, M, 59
squeezed middle 63
star performers 34
stock-exchange-focused financing 70
Storey, J. 33
strategic human resource management
    (SHRM) 4–5, 10–11; business
    life-cycle, linking to 15;
    business strategy, linking to
    14–15; changing contexts of
    62–74; definition of 6; fit,
    flexibility. and agility and
    75–87; future of 88–97; HR
    competences and 48–61;
    importance of 13–14; major
    variables of concern in 6–7;
    mapping field of 4–17;
    organizational strategy and
    structure, linking to 15–16;
    performance outcomes and
    16–17, 18–31; practice areas
    and 32–47
strategic partners 56
strategic positioners 53
strategy: de facto 12; emergent 12; as
    plan 11–13
strong cultures 46
Su, Z. X. 28, 78
sub-contracting 63, 70, 89
succession planning 37
Svetlik, L. 80
system strength 23, 33

Takeuchi, R. 22
talent management 41–43, 88
targeting practices 23
Taylor, M. 69, 94–95
team focus 12
technology: deskilling and 72; as driver
    of exchange 71–73; labour
    productivity and 73; skill
    requirements and 75
technology and media integrator 54, 74
Teece, D. J. 13, 82

Temin, P. 63
Testing for Competences
    (McClelland) 52
Rise of Alternative Work Arrangements
    in the United States 1995–2015
    (Katz and Krueger) 68
theory and practice 9–10
TikTok 63
Tobin, J. 59
total quality management 20
total reward 40
total reward steward 54
Trade Union Congress (TUC)
    Directory 44
training 41–42
Troth, A. 4
Truss, C. 23
Tyson, S. 49
Tzabbar, D. 26, 27

Uber 70
Ukraine 2
Ulrich, D. 6, 52, 53–55, 56, 57
unions 43–44, 65–66
United Nations Global Compact 74
United States Army Air Corps 51

value creation, waves of 59–60, *60*
varieties of capitalism 71
Venkatraman, N. 76, 79
venture capital 2
voluntarist system 66

Walton, R. E. 20

The Warehouse: Workers and Robots at
    Amazon (Delfanti) 72
Way, S. A. 22, 84–85, 86
Weick, K. 82
Weil, D. 69, 70
Weinsten, H. 32
well-being-oriented human resource
    management practices
    (WBHRM) 29
Westlake, S. 63, 64
Where's the 'Human' in Human
    Resource Management?
    Managing Work in the 21st
    Century (Gold and Smith) 3
Why We Hate HR (Hammonds) 50
Williamson, J. G. 63
Williamson, O. 59
Wilson, M. C. 19
work style 59
workers, as assets 5
workforce analytics 93
Working Backwards: Insights, Stories,
    and Secrets from Inside
    Amazon (Bryar and Carr) 72
working from home 1–2, 64, 73
Workplace Employment Relations
    Survey (WERS) 49–50
World Management Survey 6
Wright, P. M. 6, 19, 22, 24, 28, 50, 76,
    82, 83, 84, 95

Youndt, M. A. 21

zero-hour contracts 44

Printed in the United States
by Baker & Taylor Publisher Services

Printed in the United States
by Baker & Taylor Publisher Services